The Man Called Peter

Commentary on Peter's 1st and 2nd Epistles

The Man Called Peter

Commentary on Peter's 1st and 2nd Epistles

Bob Koonce Th. D.

The Man Called Peter
Commentary on Peter's 1st and 2nd Epistles

Copyright © 2019 Bob Koonce/John Koonce

Unless otherwise identified, all scripture used are taken from the Authorized King James Version

ISBN: 9781076923271

Bob Koonce Commentary Series Book 4
Nonfiction > Religion > Biblical Commentary > New Testament
Nonfiction > Religion > Biblical Studies > New Testament

Independently Published

Printed in the United States of America

Table of Contents

Introduction

Simon Peter, the author of both First and Second Peter, was a remarkable man. He appeared prominently in the four Gospels and in the first three chapters of the Book of Acts. Simon was led to Jesus by his brother, Andrew, the latter mentioned only sparsely in Scripture. However, Peter is mentioned not only in the Gospels and Acts, but the Apostle Paul mentioned him also. Jesus gave Simon the name, Peter, meaning a rock--a name that fit him well.

Peter wrote with intimacy as of one "who had been there." The words of John 1:1, *"That which was from the beginning, which we have heard, which we have seen with our eyes, which we have looked upon, and our hands have handled, of the Word of life;"* describe him well. He wrote in a straight-forward manner, attacking problems head on, yet his advice always flavored with a passion that only a man of God could know. His words in 1Peter 2:25 *"For ye were as sheep going astray; but are now returned unto the **Shepherd** and **Bishop** of your souls,"* will be forever beautiful.

Authorship for the Book of 2 Peter provided more fuel for the fires of debate among translators than for any other Book in the New Testament. Thankfully, majority opinion prevailed and the Book was given place in the Authorized Version of the Bible. Surely, no Bible could ever be complete without the inclusion of 2 Peter.

I have read both Books by Peter numerous times during the 71 years of my walk with God, and I have experienced a feeling of being so completely blessed and awed after every reading. I feel honored in preparing and presenting a Commentary on each of the two Books. You will find them invaluable in your study of God's Word.

Bob Koonce

I - Trial of Your Faith

1 Peter, an apostle of Jesus Christ, to the strangers scattered throughout Pontus, Galatia, Cappadocia, Asia, and Bithynia,
2 Elect according to the foreknowledge of God the Father, through sanctification of the Spirit, unto obedience and sprinkling of the blood of Jesus Christ: Grace unto you, and peace, be multiplied.
3 Blessed be the God and Father of our Lord Jesus Christ, which according to his abundant mercy hath begotten us again unto a lively hope by the resurrection of Jesus Christ from the dead,
4 To an inheritance incorruptible, and undefiled, and that fadeth not away, reserved in heaven for you,
5 Who are kept by the power of God through faith unto salvation ready to be revealed in the last time.
6 Wherein ye greatly rejoice, though now for a season, if need be, ye are in heaviness through manifold temptations:
7 That the trial of your faith, being much more precious than of gold that perisheth, though it be tried with fire, might be found unto praise and honour and glory at the appearing of Jesus Christ:
8 Whom having not seen, ye love; in whom, though now ye see him not, yet believing, ye rejoice with joy unspeakable and full of glory:
9 Receiving the end of your faith, even the salvation of your souls.
10 ¶ Of which salvation the prophets have enquired and searched diligently, who prophesied of the grace that should come unto you:
11 Searching what, or what manner of time the Spirit of Christ which was in them did signify, when it testified beforehand the sufferings of Christ, and the glory that should follow.
12 Unto whom it was revealed, that not unto themselves, but unto us they did minister the things, which are now reported unto you by them that have preached the gospel unto you with the Holy Ghost sent down from heaven; which things the angels desire to look into.
13 Wherefore gird up the loins of your mind, be sober, and hope to the end for the grace that is to be brought unto you at the revelation of Jesus Christ;
14 As obedient children, not fashioning yourselves according to the former lusts in your ignorance:

15 But as he which hath called you is holy, so be ye holy in all manner of conversation;
16 Because it is written, Be ye holy; for I am holy.
17 And if ye call on the Father, who without respect of persons judgeth according to every man's work, pass the time of your sojourning here in fear:
18 Forasmuch as ye know that ye were not redeemed with corruptible things, as silver and gold, from your vain conversation received by tradition from your fathers;
19 But with the precious blood of Christ, as of a lamb without blemish and without spot:
20 Who verily was foreordained before the foundation of the world, but was manifest in these last times for you,
21 Who by him do believe in God, that raised him up from the dead, and gave him glory; that your faith and hope might be in God.
22 Seeing ye have purified your souls in obeying the truth through the Spirit unto unfeigned love of the brethren, see that ye love one another with a pure heart fervently:
23 Being born again, not of corruptible seed, but of incorruptible, by the word of God, which liveth and abideth forever.
24 For all flesh is as grass, and all the glory of man as the flower of grass. The grass withereth, and the flower thereof falleth away:
25 But the word of the Lord endureth for ever. And this is the word which by the gospel is preached unto you.

The prophets wrote as the Spirit of God moved them—as it touched them; Peter wrote as would a man who had personally walked with Jesus Christ. It is impossible to understand this book with a carnal mind. Even a person who has been redeemed by the Power of God through the blood of Jesus Christ, still must study in *"rightly dividing the word of truth"* (2Timothy 2:15).

There is an enriching of the spirit of a person to be gained in reading either or both of Peter's writings. There is a conviction that this man had indeed been blessed with a very personal knowledge of the Lord Jesus; a knowledge that flowed into each word he wrote. I have read both his books numerous times over the years. I've yet to close a reading without feeling the disappointment that he had not written more.
1 Peter, an apostle of Jesus Christ, to the strangers scattered

throughout Pontus, Galatia, Cappadocia, Asia, and Bithynia,
Peter, meaning "a stone, rock, or cliff" was the surname given by Jesus to Simon, brother of Andrew, both fishermen. Simon was one of the earliest of the chosen disciples of the Lord. He is better known as Peter, his surname, than by Simon, his given name. His surname is used in both books attributed to him.

Peter introduced himself to **strangers** relocated to cities in what is known today as western Turkey. It was necessary that the author of the epistle be identified, for many of the recipients of his letter possibly knew Peter not at all. He identified himself as an apostle of Jesus Christ, not to boast, but to establish the credence of what he wrote.

The word, **strangers**, now and for years gone by, offers debate material for Bible students, laymen, and scholars. Some think the word speaks of Jews driven from Israel by Babylon, or later, by Rome. Others think it identifies Christians driven from Rome at the time of Aquila and Priscilla's expulsion from Italy along with all other Jews.

The word "strangers" is used in Hebrews 11:1, in 1 Peter 2:11, called "pilgrims" there, and in this verse--only 3 times in the New Testament. It does not carry the connotation of "being strange, odd." It properly identifies people permanently dwelling (not merely visiting) in a place where they wouldn't have dwelt except for extenuating circumstances. Verse 2 renders a more definite definition for the word as it is written in this verse.

2 Elect according to the foreknowledge of God the Father, through sanctification of the Spirit, unto obedience and sprinkling of the blood of Jesus Christ: Grace unto you, and peace, be multiplied.

"Strangers" so-named in verse 1, are called "Elect" in this verse 2. With this, we are able to positively determine that "strangers" and "elect" are the same in meaning, and identify the same people.

Unlike mortal men, God does not and did not present answers when questions arose. From the beginning—*In the beginning* (Gen. 1:1) God determined everything. Isa. 46:10: *Declaring the end from the beginning, and from ancient times the things that are not yet done, saying, My counsel shall stand, and I will do all my pleasure:* From the **very beginning** the **Elect** was determined.

Scripture identifies New Testament believers as the Elect.

Second Thessalonians 2:13: *But **we** are bound to give thanks alway to God for you, **brethren** beloved of the Lord, because God **from the beginning hath chosen you** (Gentiles) **to salvation** through sanctification of the Spirit and belief of the truth:*

Paul wrote the preceding verse to Gentile converts at Thessalonica. **From the beginning**, the Thessalonian believers were chosen to be the Elect, the Election of God as also were the Colossians believers: Colossians 3:12: *Put on therefore, as the **elect of God**, holy and beloved, bowels of mercies, kindness, humbleness of mind, meekness, longsuffering;*

1Thess. 1:4: *Knowing, brethren beloved, your **election** of God.*

There is but **one Elect**, and it has been so **from the beginning**.
3 Blessed be the God and Father of our Lord Jesus Christ, which according to his abundant mercy hath begotten us again unto a lively hope by the resurrection of Jesus Christ from the dead,

God and Father of our Lord Jesus Christ: Not **God** and a **Father.** There is but one God! **God** (deity); **Father** (deity); **Lord** (deity); **Jesus** (human); **Christ** (deity in Jesus-God human). Adam was made in the pattern of Jesus (Romans 5:14). Adam was made body and spirit. The Lord Jesus, who is the pattern after which Adam was made, was comprised of Spirit and body. He was God (Spirit) in a man.

2 Corinthians. 5:19: *To wit, that God was in Christ, reconciling the world unto himself, not imputing their trespasses unto them; and hath committed unto us the word of reconciliation.*
Colossians 2:9: *For in him (Jesus) dwelleth all the fulness of the Godhead bodily.* The **Father** and **Son--One Entity**.

…. hath begotten us again: Begotten—born—he has born,

rebirthed us. Jesus spoke of this in John 3:5,6: *⁵ Jesus answered, Verily, verily, I say unto thee, Except a man be born of water and of the Spirit, he cannot enter into the kingdom of God. ⁶ That which is born of the flesh is flesh; and that which is born of the Spirit is spirit.*

The New Birth cannot be earned, bought, or bartered. Titus 3:5 states: *Not by works of righteousness which we have done, but according to his mercy he saved us, by the washing of regeneration, and renewing of the Holy Ghost; ....* and *hath* **begotten** *us* **again** *unto a lively hope* **by the resurrection of Jesus Christ from** *the dead.*

4 To an inheritance incorruptible, and undefiled, and that fadeth not away, reserved in heaven for you,

To an inheritance—an incorruptible, undefiled, never-ending, inherited crown reserved in heaven. Inheritances can't be earned or gained by thriftiness. These are gifts from benefactors, usually parents, near relatives, or some other generous source. But all earthly inheritances are corruptible and defiled in some way or another. They are never eternal.

5 Who are kept by the power of God through faith unto salvation ready to be revealed in the last time.

Who are kept by the power of God: The pronoun "who" here refers to *Elect according to the foreknowledge of God*--verse 2—the New Testament Church. See my comments under that verse.

Who are kept: In Peter's second epistle, chapter 1, verse 4, Peter penned the words "exceeding great and precious promises." God is jealous for His children. He does not redeem souls to cut them adrift to flounder on their own. *"Fear not, little children,"* and *"Yea, I am with you alway,"* poignantly describe the love of God. My testimony is but 1 in the millions that could be offered, but at 89 years of age and after a 71-year walk with God, He has yet to fail me. He never has—He never will!

6 Wherein ye greatly rejoice, though now for a season, if need be, ye are in heaviness through manifold temptations:

I think the verse delivers the message: *⁶now for a season-- ye greatly rejoice*(d)-- *⁵Who are kept by the power of God-- ⁶for a season... are in heaviness through manifold temptations:*

It must be remembered that Peter wrote this epistle, this letter, to *the strangers* (Christians) *scattered throughout Pontus, Galatia, Cappadocia, Asia, and Bithynia.* His letter was not intended to be read only in churches in that area, but that his writings be read to or by all Christians there. While some areas enjoyed peace and quiet, other areas may have been subjected to great distress.

7 That the trial of your faith, being much more precious than of gold that perisheth, though it be tried with fire, might be found unto praise and honour and glory at the appearing of Jesus Christ:

Gold, the only metal that will not tarnish, is ridded of foreign materials by fire. Gold wears away over time through usage—faith increases through usage—trials, tribulations, unreasonable hardships, etc. increases faith in size and effectiveness—faith is *more precious than gold.*

....be found unto praise and honour and glory at the appearing of Jesus Christ: Peter **slept**, chained to 2 guards the night before his scheduled execution; Stephen died under the hail of rocks, praying for his executioners; John wrote the Book of Revelation as a prisoner on Patmos isle; Paul and Silas sang to the Lord at midnight in a black, deplorable jail, their backs beaten to bloody messes—all of it **unto praise and honour and glory at the appearing of Jesus Christ!** And all that to glorify the Lord, Jesus Christ.

8 Whom having not seen, ye love; in whom, though now ye see him not, yet believing, ye rejoice with joy unspeakable and full of glory:

Belief (faith) is the vehicle that lifts the paralytic from his wheel chair to dance like a child; the vehicle that causes the blind to see, the dumb to talk, the deaf to hear, and the dead to climb from their coffins. It is the power and hope of the martyr, the sinner to be free from his sin, and the hope of every saint to be unshackled from the grip of gravity to rise and meet the Lord Jesus in the clouds when He comes for His saints!

9 Receiving the end of your faith, even the salvation of your souls.

I rearranged this verse as I believe it should read:
Receiving the salvation of your souls--the end of your faith.

Faith produces salvation, and salvation produces faith. The verse is truth in its original print, yet the rearranged version produces the same message in a less-complicated arrangement.

Romans 6:22 delivers the same message in another arrangement:
*But now being made free from sin, and become servants to God, ye have your fruit unto holiness, and the **end** everlasting life.*

I borrow the following excerpt from the Jamieson-Fausset-Brown commentary:

"Receiving — in sure anticipation; 'the end of your faith,' that is, its crowning consummation, finally completed 'salvation' (Peter here confirms Paul's teaching as to *justification by faith*): also receiving *now* the title to it and the first-fruits of it. In 1Peter 1:10 the 'salvation' is represented as *already present,* whereas 'the prophets' had it not as yet present. It must, therefore, in this verse, refer to the present: *Deliverance now from a state of wrath:* believers even now 'receive salvation,' though its full 'revelation' is future.

10 Of which salvation the prophets have enquired and searched diligently, who prophesied of the grace that should come unto you:

Clarke's Commentary:

"Of which salvation the prophets have inquired - The incarnation and suffering of Jesus Christ, and the redemption procured by him for mankind, were made known, in a general way, by the prophets; but they themselves did not know the time when these things were to take place, nor the people among and by whom he was to suffer, etc.; they therefore inquired accurately or earnestly, εξεζητησαν, and searched diligently, εξηρευνησαν, inquiring of others who were then under the same inspiration, and carefully searching the writings of those who had, before their time, spoken of these things. The prophets plainly saw that the grace which was to come under the Messiah's kingdom was vastly superior to anything that had ever been exhibited under the law; and in consequence they made all possible inquiry, and searched as after grains of gold, hidden among sand or compacted with ore, (for such is the meaning of the original word), in order to ascertain the time, and the signs of that time, in which this wondrous display of God's love and mercy to man was to take place; but all that God thought fit to instruct them in was what is mentioned in 1Peter 1:12."

11 Searching what, or what manner of time the Spirit of Christ which was in them did signify, when it testified beforehand the sufferings of Christ, and the glory that should follow.
Searching **what**, *or* (how) *what manner of time* (when) *the Spirit of Christ.... did signify* (did tell them). In the previous verse 11, it is written *the Spirit of Christ which was* **in them.** 2Peter 1:21 states: *For the prophecy came not in old time by the will of man: but holy men of God spake* **as they were moved by** *the Holy Ghost.* "In them" or "moved by" the Spirit offers no biblical difficulty. It does contradict modern interpretations that Old Testament prophets did not contain the Spirit within them. They did not experience the baptism of the Holy Ghost, *for the Holy Ghost was not yet given* (John 7:39).

12 Unto whom it was revealed, that not unto themselves, but unto us they did minister the things, which are now reported unto you by them that have preached the gospel unto you with the Holy Ghost sent down from heaven; which things the angels desire to look into.

Unto whom.... We are not left to wonder nor guess the meaning of these words. The answer is found in Hebrews 11:13, which vividly describes the Old Testament prophets as being the subject of **Unto whom**: *These all died in faith, not having received the promises, but having seen them afar off, and were persuaded of them, and embraced them, and confessed that they were strangers and pilgrims on the earth.*

.... the angels desire to look into: I find it hard to imagine any explanation of this phrase as being more vivid than the following description by Adam Clarke:
"**Angels desire to look into**. parakuqai. To stoop down to; the

posture of those who are earnestly intent on finding out a thing, especially a writing difficult to be read; they bring it to the light, place it so that the rays may fall on it as collectively as possible, and then stoop down in order to examine all the parts, that they may be able to make out the whole. There is evidently an allusion here to the attitude of the cherubim who stood at the ends of the ark of the covenant, in the inner tabernacle, with their eyes turned towards the mercy-seat or propitiatory in a bending posture, as if looking attentively, or, as we term it, poring upon it. Even the holy angels are struck with astonishment at the plan of human redemption, and justly wonder at the **incarnation** of that **infinite** object of their adoration. If then these things be objects of deep consideration to the angels of God, how much more so should they be to us; in them angels can have no such interest as human beings have."

13 Wherefore gird up the loins of your mind, be sober, and hope to the end for the grace that is to be brought unto you at the revelation of Jesus Christ;

Wherefore: Faced with such evidence of that which has been just given, action is now demanded-g*ird up the loins of your mind.* Loins, as most adults must know, is the organ of reproduction. It is so intended in this phrase. A Christian is not saved to simply vegetate; he/she is saved to create, to reproduce. And verse 14 presents a pattern of how that creation should be done:

*14 **As obedient children**, not fashioning yourselves according to the former lusts in your ignorance:*
15 But as he which hath called you is holy, so be ye holy in all manner of conversation;
16 Because it is written, Be ye holy; for I am holy.

As obedient children: James 3:18 states: *…. the fruit of righteousness is sown in peace of them that make peace.* Eph. 5:9 gives this: *(For the fruit of the Spirit is in all goodness and righteousness and truth.* Galatians 5:22 gives a third witness to the fruit that **obedient children** will produce: *But the fruit of the Spirit is love, joy, peace, longsuffering, gentleness, goodness, faith,*
17 And if ye call on the Father, who without respect of persons judgeth according to every man's work, pass the time of your

sojourning here in fear:

I believe this verse could be better understood rearranged to read: *And if ye.... pass the time of your sojourning here in fear, ye call on the Father, who without respect of persons judgeth according to every man's work....* The verse is incomplete whether as in the original writing or as the rearranged verse puts it. Its completion can be accomplished **only** if it is attached to the remaining verses of this chapter.

I think my reader will understand the arranged verses better, and will agree with the message the rearranged verses deliver. Following the rearrangement, I leave verses 17-25 as they are printed in the KJV Bible.

[17]And if ye.... pass the time of your sojourning here in fear, ye call on the Father, who without respect of persons judgeth according to every man's work, [18] Forasmuch as ye know that ye were not redeemed from your vain conversation with corruptible things, as (like) silver and gold, (corruptible things) received by tradition from your fathers, [19] But with the precious blood of Christ, as of a lamb without blemish and without spot:[20] Who verily was foreordained before the foundation of the world, but was manifest in these last times for you,
21 Who (You) by him do believe in God, that raised him up from the dead, and gave him glory; that your faith and hope might be in God. [22] Seeing ye have purified your souls in obeying the truth through the Spirit unto unfeigned love of the brethren, [23] Being born again, not of corruptible seed, but of incorruptible, by the word of God, which liveth and abideth for ever; **see that ye love one another with a pure heart fervently:**

Now, if we connect the rearranged verse 17 with the bolded words of verse 23, we have *And if ye.... pass the time of your sojourning here in fear, ye call on the Father, who* **without respect** *of persons* **judgeth** *according to every man's work* **see that ye love one another with a pure heart fervently:** These last 10 words in bold print finish the thought started in verse 17.

24 For all flesh is as grass, and all the glory of man as the flower of grass. The grass withereth, and the flower thereof falleth away: ²⁵*But the word of the Lord endureth forever. And this is the word which by the gospel is preached unto you.*

Verses 17-25 in their original order in the KJV Bible:

17 And if ye call on the Father, who without respect of persons judgeth according to every man's work, pass the time of your sojourning here in fear:
18 Forasmuch as ye know that ye were not redeemed with corruptible things, as silver and gold, from your vain conversation received by tradition from your fathers;
19 But with the precious blood of Christ, as of a lamb without blemish and without spot:
20 Who verily was foreordained before the foundation of the world, but was manifest in these last times for you,
21 Who by him do believe in God, that raised him up from the dead, and gave him glory; that your faith and hope might be in God.
22 Seeing ye have purified your souls in obeying the truth through the Spirit unto unfeigned love of the brethren, see that ye love one another with a pure heart fervently:
23 Being born again, not of corruptible seed, but of incorruptible, by the word of God, which liveth and abideth forever.
24 For all flesh is as grass, and all the glory of man as the flower of grass. The grass withereth, and the flower thereof falleth away:
25 But the word of the Lord endureth for ever. And this is the word which by the gospel is preached unto you.

II - Shepherd and Bishop of the Soul

1Wherefore laying aside all malice, and all guile, and hypocrisies, and envies, and all evil speakings,
2 As newborn babes, desire the sincere milk of the word, that ye may grow thereby:
3 If so be ye have tasted that the Lord is gracious.
4 To whom coming, as unto a living stone, disallowed indeed of men, but chosen of God, and precious,
5 Ye also, as lively stones, are built up a spiritual house, an holy priesthood, to offer up spiritual sacrifices, acceptable to God by Jesus Christ.
6 Wherefore also it is contained in the scripture, Behold, I lay in Sion a chief corner stone, elect, precious: and he that believeth on him shall not be confounded.
7 Unto you therefore which believe he is precious: but unto them which be disobedient, the stone which the builders disallowed, the same is made the head of the corner,
8 And a stone of stumbling, and a rock of offence, even to them which stumble at the word, being disobedient: whereunto also they were appointed.
9 But ye are a chosen generation, a royal priesthood, an holy nation, a peculiar people; that ye should shew forth the praises of him who hath called you out of darkness into his marvellous light:
10 Which in time past were not a people, but are now the people of God: which had not obtained mercy, but now have obtained mercy.
11 Dearly beloved, I beseech you as strangers and pilgrims, abstain from fleshly lusts, which war against the soul;
12 Having your conversation honest among the Gentiles: that, whereas they speak against you as evildoers, they may by your good works, which they shall behold, glorify God in the day of visitation.
13 Submit yourselves to every ordinance of man for the Lord's sake: whether it be to the king, as supreme;
14 Or unto governors, as unto them that are sent by him for the punishment of evildoers, and for the praise of them that do well.
15 For so is the will of God, that with well doing ye may put to

silence the ignorance of foolish men:
16 As free, and not using your liberty for a cloke of maliciousness, but as the servants of God.
17 Honour all men. Love the brotherhood. Fear God. Honour the king.
18 Servants, be subject to your masters with all fear; not only to the good and gentle, but also to the froward.
19 For this is thankworthy, if a man for conscience toward God endure grief, suffering wrongfully.
20 For what glory is it, if, when ye be buffeted for your faults, ye shall take it patiently? but if, when ye do well, and suffer for it, ye take it patiently, this is acceptable with God.
21 For even hereunto were ye called: because Christ also suffered for us, leaving us an example, that ye should follow his steps:
22 Who did no sin, neither was guile found in his mouth:
23 Who, when he was reviled, reviled not again; when he suffered, he threatened not; but committed himself to him that judgeth righteously:
24 Who his own self bare our sins in his own body on the tree, that we, being dead to sins, should live unto righteousness: by whose stripes ye were healed.
25 For ye were as sheep going astray; but are now returned unto the Shepherd and Bishop of your souls.

It is too easy and too tempting to criticize the work of others who accomplished the very thing that we endeavor to accomplish. However, the division of Scripture into chapters and verses has created much confusion over the years. Thoughts are frequently divided into separate verses and into separate chapters. Throughout chapter 1, Peter set forth the excellences of the Word of God, calling it incorruptible and eternal. That thought is carried on into this chapter as we can see in the first word, "wherefore."

1Wherefore laying aside all malice, and all guile, and hypocrisies, and envies, and all evil speakings,
2 As newborn babes, desire the sincere milk of the word, that ye may grow thereby:

The introductory word, **wherefore**, for verse 1 gives the same connotation that the conjunction, **and**, renders. To demonstrate my point, I insert the last verse of chapter 1 here and add, wherefore, the first word in this chapter:

1:25:But the word of the Lord endureth for ever. And this is the word which by the gospel is preached unto you—wherefore....

By his inserting "wherefore" as the first word in verse 1 of this chapter, Peter's intent for the verse could be worded: "**And**, due to the fact that *the word of the Lord endureth for ever, lay aside all malice, and all guile, and hypocrisies, and envies, and all evil speakings."*

Wherefore: Continuing from his prior exhortation, Peter named the evils they needed to shed: all ***malice***, all ***guile***, *and* **hypocrisies**, *and* **envies**, *and* all ***evil speakings*** (evil conversations—gossip) *as newborn babies desire the sincere milk of the word.* How clean, how freed, how uncluttered a person would feel after having discarded these 5 evils!

2 As newborn babes, desire the sincere milk of the word, that ye may grow thereby:
3 If so be ye have tasted that the Lord is gracious.

Peter's flowing penmanship in this Book is so admirable. Coupled with the smooth style of his writing is the evidence of a personal relationship with his Lord, Jesus Christ. The rough, impetuous fisherman had been converted to a powerful apostle and witness for a resurrected, living Lord Jesus Christ.

Peter was very aware that the Strangers, the Elect, to whom he wrote were not perfect, were not yet finished. (Strangers and Elect are discussed and identified under verses 1 and 2 of the previous chapter.) He, formerly, had been guilty of the same faults they experienced, but had been born again. Thus, he urged them to *"desire the sincere milk of the word, that ye may grow thereby."* **But**, he asserted, they could grow only if *"ye have tasted that the Lord is gracious* (verse 3).

In Matthew 18:2,3, we have the words: *²And Jesus called a little child unto him, and set him in the midst of them, ³And said, Verily I say unto you, Except ye be converted, and become as little children, ye shall not enter into the kingdom of heaven.*

From Jamieson-Fausset-Brown:

"To guileless feeding on the word by the sense of their privileges as new-born babes, living stones in the spiritual temple built on Christ the chief corner-stone, and royal priests, in contrast to their former state: also to abstinence from fleshly lusts, and to walk worthily in all relations of life, so that the world without which opposes them may be constrained to glorify God in seeing their good works. Christ, the grand pattern to follow in patience under suffering for well-doing."

4 To whom coming, as unto a living stone, disallowed indeed of men, but chosen of God, and precious,

*To **whom coming**—*Jesus---*a **living stone**—*Jesus---***disallowed*** (rejected) *of **men**---*Jesus---***but chosen of God, and precious!*** *Therefore, let all the house of Israel know assuredly, that God hath made that same Jesus, whom ye have crucified, both Lord and Christ--*Acts 2:36—a message preached on the Day of Pentecost by the same man who wrote this epistle—Peter!

5 Ye also, as lively stones, are built up a spiritual house, an holy priesthood, to offer up spiritual sacrifices, acceptable to God by Jesus Christ.

***Ye also*---**those to whom he wrote; the strangers (chapter 1, verses 1 and 2 comments), the Christians that he didn't know by name in those cities.

….***as lively stones:*** (living stones) takes their" meaning from *a living stone* in verse 4, the **stone** being Jesus Christ, of course. From mortal, human beings, the **living Stone, Jesus**, builds a spiritual house of believers.

---***are built up a spiritual house:*** Ephesians, chapter 2, verses 18-22, speaks of this spiritual house:

Eph 2:18: *For through him we both have access by one Spirit unto the Father.*

2:19: Now therefore ye are no more strangers and foreigners, but fellow-citizens with the saints, and of the household of God;

2:20 And are built upon the foundation of the apostles and prophets, Jesus Christ himself being the chief corner stone;

2:21 In whom all the building fitly framed together groweth unto an holy temple in the Lord:

2:22 In whom ye also are builded together for an habitation of God through the Spirit.

The author of Hebrews gave the following explanation for "a spiritual house."
*But Christ as a son over his own house; **whose house are we**, if we hold fast the confidence and the rejoicing of the hope firm unto the end* (Heb. 3:6).

...an holy priesthood: *For the priesthood being changed, there is made of necessity a change also of the law* (Heb. 7:12). Priests under the Mosaic Law needed not be spiritual; actually, some of them appear as having been rather wicked. The Law contained no demand that a man repent of his sins. The office of priest was acquired by birth from a priest father. Similarly, a New Testament priest inherits the office via the New Birth. It is a holy birth that results in **an holy priesthood**.

Bear in mind the very import fact that the **living stone, Jesus** is the foundation for, and the source from which the **spiritual house** and the **holy priesthood** are derived. *For other foundation can no man lay than that is laid, which is Jesus Christ* (1Cor. 3:11).

....to offer up spiritual sacrifices: This phrase is clearly interpreted in Romans 12:1:
I beseech you therefore, brethren, by the mercies of God, that ye present your bodies a <u>living</u> <u>sacrifice</u>, holy, acceptable unto God, which is your reasonable service.

*6 **Wherefore** also it is contained in the scripture, Behold, I lay in Sion **a chief corner stone**, elect, precious: and he that believeth on* *him shall not be confounded.*

Isaiah 28:16 gives a nearly identical wording for this verse: *Therefore, thus saith the Lord GOD, Behold, I lay in Zion for a foundation a stone, a tried stone, a precious corner stone, a sure foundation: he that believeth shall not make haste.*

The word "wherefore" is treated earlier in this epistle, yet I find its use here again somewhat interesting. **Wherefore** in this verse 6 is followed by the word "therefore" in the next verse. Peter used "wherefore" in the sense of saying, "In addition to what I've already written, Scripture also confirms me with the words, *'Behold, I lay in Sion a chief corner stone, elect, precious: and he that believeth on him shall not be confounded.'*"

Therefore, in the next verse, conveys the thought, "Now, since you have received all this added evidence, and you already counted the Lord Jesus to be precious, be blessed with further confirmation that your faith is well-placed."

*7 Unto you **therefore** which believe he is precious: but unto them which be disobedient, the stone which the builders disallowed, the same is made the head of the corner,*

.... the stone which the builders disallowed: The **stone** mentioned here is Jesus. The word, **builders,** indicates the Jewish priests, Levites, scribes, lawyers, religious parties, and others of the Jewish elite that refused to accept Jesus as their Messiah. In the first chapter of the Gospel of John, verse 11, we have these words: He *came unto his own, and his own received him not.* How tragic! In Matthew 21:42, Jesus demanded: *"Did ye never read in the scriptures, The **stone** which the **builders rejected**, the same is become the **head of the corner**: this is the Lord's doing, and it is marvellous in our eyes?*

.... the same is made the head of the corner: In a masonry building, the corner stone is the most important stone in the entire structure, for to it the whole structure is tuned. Without it, the whole building could not be tuned, and the finished product might well be far amiss from the original intent. Ephesians 2:20 states: *And are* *built upon the foundation of the apostles and prophets,* **Jesus Christ** *himself being the* **chief** *corner stone.* He, Jesus, is the **head** of the corner.

Clarke's Commentary supplies the following information:

"Behold, I lay in Sion - This intimates that the foundation of the Christian Church should be laid at Jerusalem; and there it was laid, for there Christ suffered, and there the preaching of the Gospel commenced.

"A chief corner stone - This is the same as the foundation stone; and it is called here the chief corner stone because it is laid in the foundation, at an angle of the building where its two sides form the groundwork of a side and end wall. And this might probably be designed to show that, in Jesus, both Jews and Gentiles were to be united; and this is probably the reason why it was called a stone of stumbling, and rock of offense; for nothing stumbled, nothing offended the Jews so much as the calling of the Gentiles into the Church of God, and admitting them to the same privileges which had been before peculiar to the Jews."

8 And a stone of stumbling, and a rock of offence, even to them which stumble at the word, being disobedient: whereunto also they were appointed.

Romans 9:32,33 speak of the stumbling stone: *32 Wherefore? Because they sought it not by faith, but as it were by the works of the law. For they stumbled at that stumblingstone; 33 As it is written, Behold, I lay in Sion a stumblingstone and rock of offence: and whosoever believeth on him shall not be ashamed.* Christian readers have no problem understanding that the **stumbling stone** refers to Jesus.

.... whereunto also they were appointed. This word, **appointed**, refers more to a time period than it does to people. God knows the end from the beginning, and He knows who will accept Him, and who will not. Yet, in His great mercy, He allows a cursing infidel to continue cursing. God is in no rush--judgment doesn't come until after death. From the beginning, God knew all those who would reject the Savior, the Rock of offence, but he allowed them to live and scheme until Jesus' trial and death. It was at that moment that

they **appointed** themselves to be the voice of the people, and they demanded the Lord's death.

9 But ye are a chosen generation, a royal priesthood, an holy nation, a peculiar people; that ye should shew forth the praises of him who hath called you out of darkness into his marvellous light:
10 Which in time past were not a people, but are now the people of God: which had not obtained mercy, but now have obtained mercy.

*…. **a chosen generation, a royal priesthood, an holy nation, a peculiar people*** (verse 9). What rich, poignant language to describe the Gentile children of God!

Verses 9 and 10 must be considered together. Verse 10 tells us that the people of verse 9 (Gentiles) were not formerly a people, i.e., people who had been given the Word of God, thus, they had not been given the hope of salvation. But by having gained salvation through Jesus Christ, they were then a people—**a chosen generation**. The word, **generation**, should be understood as "a group" and not as "a period of time".

11 Dearly beloved, I beseech you as strangers and pilgrims, abstain from fleshly lusts, which war against the soul;
Dearly beloved: The 2 words here refer to the expression, *Which in time past were not a people* (Gentiles) in verse 10.

Strangers and pilgrims in this verse are the same as those which are discussed and defined in comments on verses 1 and 2 of chapter 1. The comments there identify these two as being the same, and that they refer to Christians scattered throughout the southwester portion of today's Turkey.

I beseech you as strangers and pilgrims: "Oh, Christian Gentiles, you indeed are strangers and pilgrims in your own world!"
*…. **abstain from fleshly lusts:*** "Don't surrender to the same sinful lusts that formerly enslaved you."

12 Having your conversation honest among the Gentiles: that, whereas they speak against you as evildoers, they may by your good works, which they shall behold, glorify God in the day of visitation.

....in the day of visitation: The word, visitation, is used several times throughout the Old Testament, and is used variously to mean judgment or death. Luke 19:44 uses the word to describe the capture and destruction of Jerusalem in A.D. 70: *And shall lay thee even with the ground, and thy children within thee; and they shall not leave in thee one stone upon another; because thou knewest not the time of thy* **visitation.**

I think "visitation" might be understood if the verse were to be rearranged thus: *They shall behold your good works and shall glorify God in the day of* (their) *visitation.* I include here another commentator's thoughts on the subject that closely parallels mine:

"that they may, by your good works which they shall behold, glorify God in the day of visitation; or 'trial', or 'examination', as the Syriac version renders it; which may be understood either of human or divine visitation; if of the former, then the sense is, let the saints attend to all the duties of civil life, that when Heathen magistrates come to visit their several districts, and inquire and examine into the conduct of men, and seeing and finding that the Christians behave well and orderly, instead of persecuting them, they will bless God that they are such good subjects; if of divine visitation, which seems most likely, this must either design a visitation by way of judgment, or of mercy; for as the Jews say (d), there is פקידה, 'a visitation', for good, and a visitation for evil: God sometimes visits in a way of punishment for sin, and sometimes in a way of grace, for the good and welfare of men; and then the sense is, that when wicked men take notice of and observe the good works of the saints, their civil, honest, and orderly conversation, they shall glorify God on that account, who has enabled them to perform them; and acknowledge the goodness of them, and the wrong judgment they have passed upon them, and the ill measure they have measured out to them; and this will be, either when God visits them in a way of wrath, as at the day of judgment, or at the time of some temporal calamity before, or when he visits them in a way of mercy, calls them by his grace, and effectually works upon them by his Spirit: the same argument for the performance of good works is used by Christ, in Matt. 5:16." (Gill)
13 Submit yourselves to every ordinance of man for the Lord's sake: whether it be to the king, as supreme;

14 Or unto governors, as unto them that are sent by him for the punishment of evildoers, and for the praise of them that do well.

Submit yourselves to <u>every</u> ordinance: An exemption from a blanket-application of this phrase would be that a Christian must **not** submit to any ordinance, government, or person that demands anyone to worship or behave in any manner that disobeys and defies the Christian's God as being the only true God. Being free in Christ does not exempt a Christian from obeying the law of the land, however. Preachers and other Christians often brag that they never obey speed limits, and then refuse to accept blame by laughing over the admission. Speed limits are laws. Civil disobedience is in direct conflict with God's precepts.   Listen up, O Christian; *Submit yourselves to every ordinance of man **for the Lord's sake.** [15] For so is the will of God, that with well doing ye may put to silence the ignorance of foolish men:*

*16 As free, and not using your liberty for a cloke of maliciousness, but as the **servants** of God.*
17 Honour all men. Love the brotherhood. Fear God. Honour the king.

18 Servants, be subject to your masters with all fear; not only to the good and gentle, but also to the froward.

Servants and slaves are synonymous terms in the majority of places where "servant" is used throughout the Bible. A hired servant was not a slave, unless he/she was a servant to another owner who hired the servant to someone other than himself. As unreasonable as it may seem in a democratic society, the Bible does not condemn slavery.   The Mosaic Law contains numerous instructions concerning the buying and selling of slaves; such as: persons who could or could not be owned; treatment of; and duration periods of ownership for the various classes of slaves. Even in this verse 18, a New Testament verse, Peter wrote advice to slaves. However that may all be; slavery is a scab on the souls of men.

Gill penned an interesting opinion on the subject of servants:
"**Servants, be subject to your masters**.... This was another notion of the Jews, that because they were the seed of Abraham, they ought

not to be the servants of any; and particularly such as were believers in Christ thought they ought not to serve unbelieving masters, nor indeed believing ones, because they were equally brethren in Christ with them; hence the Apostle Peter, here, as the Apostle Paul frequently elsewhere, inculcates this duty of servants to their masters."

The remaining verses of this chapter through verse 24 deliver the message: that like as Christ suffered wrongly to provide redemption for all who will believe, so do His servants portray Him when they suffer wrongly. I've rearranged the words of the next verse as I think they should appear. *For if a man endure grief, suffering wrongfully for conscience toward God, this is thankworthy.*

19 For this is thankworthy, if a man for conscience toward God endure grief, suffering wrongfully.
20 For what glory is it, if, when ye be buffeted for your faults, ye shall take it patiently? but if, when ye do well, and suffer for it, ye take it patiently, this is acceptable with God.
21 For even hereunto were ye called: because Christ also suffered for us, leaving us an example, that ye should follow his steps:
22 Who did no sin, neither was guile found in his mouth:
23 Who, when he was reviled, reviled not again; when he suffered, he threatened not; but committed himself to him that judgeth righteously:
24 Who his own self bare our sins in his own body on the tree, that we, being dead to sins, should live unto righteousness: by whose stripes ye were healed.

25 For ye were as sheep going astray; but are now returned unto the Shepherd and Bishop of your souls.

In my opinion, verse 25 sees few passages that surpass it in sheer beauty throughout the Word of God! I am a Gentile, saved by the precious blood of the Lamb of God. Adam led us all astray from God; Abraham brought us faith; Moses' Law segregated the Jews as a chosen people, but the blood of Jesus Christ melded us all together as one by faith, Jews and Gentiles, one in the Body of Christ. I am a Gentile granted grace by the cross on which our Lord suffered to bring us all back Him.

I am a Gentile that went astray, but I *returned unto the Shepherd and Bishop of my* soul---hallelujah!

Jesus--the Lamb of God for sinners slain!

III - Hidden Man of the Heart

1 Likewise, ye wives, be in subjection to your own husbands; that, if any obey not the word, they also may without the word be won by the conversation of the wives;

2 While they behold your chaste conversation coupled with fear.

3 Whose adorning let it not be that outward adorning of plaiting the hair, and of wearing of gold, or of putting on of apparel;

4 But let it be the hidden man of the heart, in that which is not corruptible, even the ornament of a meek and quiet spirit, which is in the sight of God of great price.

5 For after this manner in the old time the holy women also, who trusted in God, adorned themselves, being in subjection unto their own husbands:

6 Even as Sara obeyed Abraham, calling him lord: whose daughters ye are, as long as ye do well, and are not afraid with any amazement.

7 Likewise, ye husbands, dwell with them according to knowledge, giving honour unto the wife, as unto the weaker vessel, and as being heirs together of the grace of life; that your prayers be not hindered.

8 Finally, be ye all of one mind, having compassion one of another, love as brethren, be pitiful, be courteous:

9 Not rendering evil for evil, or railing for railing: but contrariwise blessing; knowing that ye are thereunto called, that ye should inherit a blessing.

10 For he that will love life, and see good days, let him refrain his tongue from evil, and his lips that they speak no guile:

11 Let him eschew evil, and do good; let him seek peace, and ensue it.

12 For the eyes of the Lord are over the righteous, and his ears are open unto their prayers: but the face of the Lord is against them that do evil.

13 And who is he that will harm you, if ye be followers of that which is good?

14 But and if ye suffer for righteousness' sake, happy are ye: and be not afraid of their terror, neither be troubled;
15 But sanctify the Lord God in your hearts: and be ready always to give an answer to every man that asketh you a reason of the hope that is in you with meekness and fear:
16 Having a good conscience; that, whereas they speak evil of you, as of evildoers, they may be ashamed that falsely accuse your good conversation in Christ.
17 For it is better, if the will of God be so, that ye suffer for well doing, than for evil doing.
18 For Christ also hath once suffered for sins, the just for the unjust, that he might bring us to God, being put to death in the flesh, but quickened by the Spirit:
19 By which also he went and preached unto the spirits in prison;
20 Which sometime were disobedient, when once the longsuffering of God waited in the days of Noah, while the ark was a preparing, wherein few, that is, eight souls were saved by water.
21 The like figure whereunto even baptism doth also now save us (not the putting away of the filth of the flesh, but the answer of a good conscience toward God,) by the resurrection of Jesus Christ:
22 Who is gone into heaven, and is on the right hand of God; angels and authorities and powers being made subject unto him.

Chapter breaks: While they may have been implemented originally to perhaps give greater ease of reading and clearer understanding of Scripture, they have produced the opposite. If a first-time Bible reader were to start reading the Bible, starting with "Likewise, ye wives," the first 3 words in verse 1 of this chapter, he/she might well ask, "likewise what?" Had they not been able to read the last several verses of the previous chapter, they would be unable to make a connection. Comments following verse 1of this chapter provide information to bridge the gap between the present and previous chapter:

1 Likewise, ye wives, be in subjection to your own husbands; that, if any obey not the word, they also may without the word be won by the conversation of the wives;
2 While they behold your chaste conversation coupled with fear.

Likewise, ye wives: The previous chapter 2 dealt extensively with the subject of subjection: to governors, to kings, and to slave owners. Now, "**likewise** (as it is the case with slaves), *be in subjection to your own husbands*. The primary reason for the **subjection** here mentioned for wives, was for the purpose of winning an unbelieving husband to the Lord. Unbelieving husbands could/might be won to God by the obedience of wives **if** *".... They* (husbands) *behold your chaste conversation coupled with fear."* Fear of God produces obedience.

In heathen societies, ancient or present, girls and women were/are sometimes given no more respect than that of an animal. Until the advent of Christianity, females, young and old, were treated no better than slaves. Their lot in life became much easier, in many instances, when husbands became Christians. Even in that type situation, wives were still expected to obey their husbands.

3 Whose adorning let it not be that outward adorning of plaiting the hair, and of wearing of gold, or of putting on of apparel;
4 But let it be the hidden man of the heart, in that which is not corruptible, even the ornament of a meek and quiet spirit, which is in the sight of God of great price.

Verses 3 and 4 need rearranging to rightly convey Peter's intent. I think them better arranged thus:
Whose adorning, let it be in that which is not corruptible, even the ornament of a meek and quiet spirit--the hidden man of the heart, which is in the sight of God of great price--not that outward adorning of plaiting the hair, and of wearing of gold, or of putting on of apparel.

Peter's subject matter has yet not changed. "Whose," the first word in verse 3 is still the subject matter, and the word speaks of **wives being in subjection.** And the method whereby believing wives could/might win unbelieving husbands was by subjection, and-- *While they behold your chaste conversation coupled with fear—* they may be won.

5 For after this manner in the old time the holy women also, who trusted in God, adorned themselves, being in subjection unto their own husbands:

*For after this manner in the old time the holy women-- **adorned**
themselves, (by)**being in** subjection unto their own husbands:*

....in the old time: Having no sacred Scripture other than the
Mosaic Law and Prophets to which he could refer, Peter affirmed his
instructions to be those that **holy women** had always observed.

The words "holiness" and "modesty" are not synonyms, yet
"modesty" is often mistaken for "holiness" in "holiness"
denominations. Wicked people could dress themselves to appear
exactly like "holiness" people, yet still remain wicked. Being attired
in a manner endorsed by a religious body **does not** make the person
holy. True holiness produces modest attire—modest attire does not
produce holiness. It is essential that it be understood that from verse
1 through verse 6 of this chapter, Peter addressed **wives being
subject to their husbands**, and that's **all** he addressed in those
verses.

*6 Even as Sara obeyed Abraham, calling him lord: whose daughters
ye are, as long as ye do well, and are not afraid with any
amazement.*

Even as Sara obeyed Abraham connects directly to the instruction
in verse 1: *Likewise, **ye wives**, be in subjection to your own
husbands;*

*7 Likewise, ye husbands, dwell with them according to knowledge,
giving honour unto the wife, as unto the weaker vessel, and as being
heirs together of the grace of life; that your prayers be not hindered.*

Likewise, ye husbands: In verse 1, it is: **Likewise, ye wives.** True
marriage is a commitment, not simply a ceremony. In First
Corinthians 1:11, Paul wrote: *Nevertheless, neither is the man
without the woman, neither the woman without the man, in the Lord.*
Genesis 2:24 describes the intimate relationship of man and wife:
*Therefore shall a man leave his father and his mother, and shall
cleave unto his wife: and they shall be one flesh.*

*8 Finally, be ye all of one mind, having compassion one of another,
love as brethren, be pitiful, be courteous:*

Finally: The Apostle here seems to display weariness, and well he could have been weary when the word was penned. However, "finally" speaks more of a summation of the things he had previously written as being wholly embodied in the virtues here listed.

Compassion-love-pitiful (merciful)-**courteous:** Verse 8 is **not** a **suggestion**; it is a **command** given by Peter, and is an exact interpretation of other Scripture: I list only 2 Scriptures of the many throughout the New Testament that verify the message of this verse.
Compassion, love*:* *Be kindly affectioned one to another with brotherly love; in honour preferring one another;* (Romans 12:10) *And be ye kind one to another, tenderhearted, forgiving one another, even as God for Christ's sake hath forgiven you* (Eph. 4:32).

The Expositor's Bible concurs with my interpretation for "finally":
"The Apostle now ceases from his special admonitions, and enforces generally such qualities and conduct as must mark all who fear the Lord. 'Finally,' he says-and the word may indicate the close of his counsels; but the virtues which he inculcates are of so important a character that he may very well intend them as the apex and crown of all his previous advice – 'be ye all likeminded, compassionate, loving as brethren, tenderhearted, humble-minded.' St. Peter has here grouped together a number of epithets of which all but one are only used in the New Testament by himself, and they are of that graphic character which is so conspicuous in all the Apostle's language. 'Like-minded.' If the word be not there, the spirit is largely exemplified in the early history of the Church. How often we hear the phrase, 'with one accord,' in the opening chapters of the Acts."

Verses 9-11 contain further instruction that Peter gave in the **grouping** of instructions succeeding the word, finally, the introductory word of verse 8: I comment but briefly on these 3 verses;

9 Not rendering evil for evil, or railing for railing: but contrariwise blessing; knowing that ye are thereunto called, that ye should inherit a blessing.
In colloquial language, this verse would read: *Ye suffer evil railings*

and give blessings in return, knowing that ye shall inherit a blessing.
10 For he that will love life, and see good days, let him refrain his tongue from evil, and his lips that they speak no guile:
11 Let him eschew evil, and do good; let him seek peace, and ensue it.

I interpret these 2 verses to say, "If you desire healthy days and a long life, refrain your moth and your tongue from speaking evil and guile. Hate evil, do good things, and pursue peace.

12 For the eyes of the Lord are over the righteous, and his ears are open unto their prayers: but the face of the Lord is against them that do evil.

For the eyes of the Lord: His eyes watch *over the righteous, and his ears are open unto their prayers.* What greater blessing could anyone possibly desire than to enjoy being guarded by the God of all creation!?

.... but the face of the Lord is against them that do evil: God knows everything. He knows the thoughts of the mind before they occur. In Psalm 139:1-2, David said-- *O LORD, thou hast searched me, and known me. ²Thou knowest my downsitting and mine uprising, thou understandest my thought afar off.* **Thou knowest—** even for a Christian, those 2 words should be alarming.

13 And who is he that will harm you, if ye be followers of that which is good?
14 But and if ye suffer for righteousness' sake, happy are ye: and be not afraid of their terror, neither be troubled;

And who is he that will harm you: This is a statement, **not** a question! Romans 8:31 boldly states: *.... If God be for us, who can be against us?*   That verse, however, does not guarantee that a Christian will never suffer, as verse 14 informs us.

....and if ye suffer (verse 14) should be understood in association with Romans 8:28: *And we know that <u>all</u> things work together <u>for good</u> to them that love God, to them who are **the called** according to his purpose.*

15 But sanctify the Lord God in your hearts: and be ready always to give an answer to every man that asketh you a reason of the hope that is in you with meekness and fear:

But sanctify the Lord God in your hearts: Sanctify, "to set apart to a holy purpose" as defined by the Merriam-Webster Collegiate dictionary, certainly seems in line with the connotation of this phrase. "To sanctify your hearts with the presence of God within" seems the true intent.

16 Having a good conscience; that, whereas they speak evil of you, as of evildoers, they may be ashamed that falsely accuse your good conversation in Christ.

Having a good conscience connects with *sanctify the Lord God in your hearts* (verse 16). The Lord God in **hearts** definitely ensures a good conscience. So, despite anything that evil men might falsely accuse them, their conscience would remain a *good conscience.* Anyone suffering a bad conscience in a situation like that listed in verse 16 would have to be the accuser.

17 For it is better, if the will of God be so, that ye suffer for well doing, than for evil doing.

I interpret this verse in these words: "If the will of God permits ye to suffer for doing well, it is better that ye suffer for doing well than for doing wrong." Here again, it is necessary always to keep Romans 8:28 embedded in the soul. **All** things happen for the **good** of believers.

18 For Christ also hath once suffered for sins, the just for the unjust, that he might bring us to God, being put to death in the flesh, but quickened by the Spirit:

The love of God for sinners is so beautifully worded in John 3:16: *For God so loved the world, that he gave his only begotten Son, that whosoever believeth in him should not perish, but have everlasting life.* [17] *For God sent not his Son into the world to condemn the world; but that the world through him might be saved.* The Captain of the Christian has blazed the trail by His own suffering through the beatings during His trial before Herod, and His agony on the cross on Golgotha.

19 By which also he went and preached unto the spirits in prison;

By which-- *by the Spirit* (verse 18)- *he went and preached unto the spirits in prison.* Many, many opinions surround verse 19. I could not list all the controversies, and I will not attempt to do so. I feel it absolutely necessary to state that it is very dangerous to promote an opinion that stands in direct conflict with Scripture. I refer to one opinion that contends that Jesus' Spirit descended to hell to preach to fallen angels, hoping they would repent. That's ridiculous! In 2Peter 2:4, Scripture clearly states: *For if God spared not the angels that sinned, but cast them down to hell, and delivered them into chains of darkness, to be **reserved unto judgment**;* Jude 1:6 delivers the same message.

The Subject of Peter's discourse has not changed from verse 18, where the words--*For Christ--*, are written. The subject is still Jesus, and it is He **who**—*by the Spirit--went and preached unto the spirits in prison.* The Spirit of the man who died on Golgotha is the Spirit that descended into the lower parts of the earth.

Wherefore he saith, When he ascended up on high, he led captivity captive, and gave gifts unto men. ⁹ (Now that he ascended, what is it but that he also descended first into the lower parts of the earth? ¹⁰ He that descended is the same also that ascended up far above all heavens, that he might fill all things.) (Ephesians 4:8-11)

20 Which sometime were disobedient, when once the longsuffering of God waited in the days of Noah, while the ark was a preparing, wherein few, that is, eight souls were saved by water.

Writing styles and language usage has changed over generations, and over centuries. Sentence arrangement is different in various languages. English places the verb between the subject and the predicate, while the verb is placed afterwards in Spanish. English is not an ancient language, yet it has changed rather dramatically over years, decades, and centuries. Reading Old English is nearly as difficult as reading a related language might be. As in many other places, the King James version Bible produces misunderstanding in verse 20 due to the sentence structure. I believe disarrangement of words is the primary difficulty presented here.

I believe the verse should read: *Which were disobedient sometime(s)* (as they were disobedient) *in the days of Noah, while the ark was a preparing, wherein few, eight souls that is, were saved by water.* Any effort expended to prove there to be another chance for repentance of sins after death is wasted effort: *....it is appointed unto men **once to die,** but after this the **judgment***: (Heb. 9:27). To insist that Jesus preached **only** to the disobedient of Noah's day is an erroneous insistence.

Consider: Moses was **not** perfect; neither was David, Elijah, Elisha, Ezekiel, Daniel, or any of the great men and women in the Old Testament. They all experienced failures that could not be rescinded under the Mosaic Law. Their redemption was not possible until Jesus Christ paid the penalty for sin on the cross for all people of all time. The prophets knew that salvation would arrive in the future, but they didn't know how, when, or by Whom it would come, though they searched diligently for that answer (see 1Peter 1:10). So, until New Testament salvation became available, all the Old Testament prophets and righteous people were **prisoners** until Jesus descended to their prison and *led captivity captive* (Eph. 4:8).

21 The like figure whereunto even baptism doth also now save us (not the putting away of the filth of the flesh, but the answer of a good conscience toward God,) by the resurrection of Jesus Christ:

The like figure: For a correct understanding of the words "like figure", we must refer to verses 18 and 19 of this chapter. *.... but quickened by the Spirit* (verse. 18)*: By which* (verse 19) *also he went and preached unto the spirits in prison.* And as Jesus' body lay dead in Joseph's tomb, His Spirit descended to the *lower parts of the earth* to preached to those in death's prison. He first descended (into) and then ascended (out of)—into and out of death, setting a pattern for baptism by water.

.... whereunto even baptism doth also now save us: Men did not dictate the precepts of God's Word. Neither should they endeavor to refute it, abridge it, circumvent it, or decorate it with opposing opinions. This bolded clause at the beginning of this paragraph insists that baptism saves in like figure of Jesus' descension into and ascension from death—in and out—providing a figure (pattern) for water baptism. I insert 2 New Testament Scriptures that describe reason for water baptism:

Romans 6:4: *Therefore we are **buried with him by baptism** into death: that like as Christ was raised up from the dead by the glory of the Father, even so we also should walk in newness of life.*

Colossians 2:12: ***Buried with him in baptism,** wherein also ye are risen with him through the faith of the operation of God, who hath raised him from the dead.*

22 Who is gone into heaven, and is on the right hand of God; angels and authorities and powers being made subject unto him.

…. on the right hand of God: God is omnipresent-He is everywhere. There is no space above, below, or beside Him that He does not fill. There is no **space** unoccupied by Him; no space or place for anyone or anything to occupy. The words, **right hand**, speaks of **power**, not space or place. ***Angels and authorities and powers*** are **subject** to Him (Jesus). He is the right hand of God.

IV - What Shall the End Be?

1 Forasmuch then as Christ hath suffered for us in the flesh, arm yourselves likewise with the same mind: for he that hath suffered in the flesh hath ceased from sin;

2 That he no longer should live the rest of his time in the flesh to the lusts of men, but to the will of God.

3 For the time past of our life may suffice us to have wrought the will of the Gentiles, when we walked in lasciviousness, lusts, excess of wine, revellings, banquetings, and abominable idolatries:

4 Wherein they think it strange that ye run not with them to the same excess of riot, speaking evil of you:

5 Who shall give account to him that is ready to judge the quick and the dead.

6 For for this cause was the gospel preached also to them that are dead, that they might be judged according to men in the flesh, but live according to God in the spirit.

7 But the end of all things is at hand: be ye therefore sober, and watch unto prayer.

8 And above all things have fervent charity among yourselves: for charity shall cover the multitude of sins.

9 Use hospitality one to another without grudging.

10 As every man hath received the gift, even so minister the same one to another, as good stewards of the manifold grace of God.

11 If any man speak, let him speak as the oracles of God; if any man minister, let him do it as of the ability which God giveth: that God in all things may be glorified through Jesus Christ, to whom be praise and dominion for ever and ever. Amen.

12 Beloved, think it not strange concerning the fiery trial which is to try you, as though some strange thing happened unto you:

13 But rejoice, inasmuch as ye are partakers of Christ's sufferings; that, when his glory shall be revealed, ye may be glad also with exceeding joy.

14 If ye be reproached for the name of Christ, happy are ye; for the spirit of glory and of God resteth upon you: on their part he is evil

spoken of, but on your part he is glorified.
15 But let none of you suffer as a murderer, or as a thief, or as an evildoer, or as a busybody in other men's matters.
16 Yet if any man suffer as a Christian, let him not be ashamed; but let him glorify God on this behalf.
17 For the time is come that judgment must begin at the house of God: and if it first begin at us, what shall the end be of them that obey not the gospel of God?
18 And if the righteous scarcely be saved, where shall the ungodly and the sinner appear?
19 Wherefore let them that suffer according to the will of God commit the keeping of their souls to him in well doing, as unto a faithful Creator.

Chapter 4 opens with suffering as its subject. Peter was well acquainted with suffering; he went to great length in addressing proper arming for the saint of God to withstand the attacks of the enemy against the souls of God's people.

Young David met Goliath armed only with a sling that he beforehand had tested and proved. King Saul burdened David with armor that hampered rather than protected him, so he refused the armor. For centuries, Christian churches have endeavored to armor their parishioners with countless things that proved futile when put to ultimate tests. God *allows* His followers to be proved by persecution—what a strange way to win souls! But persecution does purify souls like fire separates metal from foreign materials that adhere to it.

John MacArthur penned a statement that I find very interesting, yet shocking at the same time: "Experts say that 200 *million* people worldwide suffer harassment, torture, and even death on a daily basis." The death knell is ringing for democratic nations over the whole earth: Dare we continue to relax?

1 Forasmuch then as Christ hath suffered for us in the flesh, arm yourselves likewise with the same mind: for he that hath suffered in the flesh hath ceased from sin;
2 That he no longer should live the rest of his time in the flesh to the lusts of men, but to the will of God.

.... Forasmuch as Christ hath suffered for us in the flesh i.e. as a human, Christ suffered in becoming a paradigm (patter) for Christians to follow.

.... arm yourselves likewise with the same mind: With the same mindset that Christ portrayed throughout His sufferings.

.... for he that hath suffered in the flesh hath ceased from sin: Spiritual caution should be employed when interpreting this clause. I think a correct interpretation would read thus: "For he (Jesus) hath suffered in the flesh and *ceased from sin*, (because he died)." Sin's temptations end at death. For the devil to attack a dedicated Christian might be likened to someone shooting a corpse. The corpse might show slight movement from the impact of the bullets, but there is no life left in a dead body-- *For ye are dead, and your life is hid with Christ in God* (Colossians 3:3).

3 For the time past of our life may suffice us to have wrought the will of the Gentiles, when we walked in lasciviousness, lusts, excess of wine, revellings, banquetings, and abominable idolatries:
4 Wherein they think it strange that ye run not with them to the same excess of riot, speaking evil of you:

For the time past of our life may suffice us: "The sins we've already committed should convince us," is the sense of this phrase. Peter linked his past to that of the Gentiles to whom he referred in this phrase. Jew or Gentile, there is no difference--*For all have sinned, and come short of the glory of God* (Romans 3:23). Definitions that follow for the sins listed in verse 3 are taken from the Merriam-Webster Collegiate Dictionary.

Lasciviousness: Lewd. Evil. Wicked.
Lusts: Personal inclination, usually intense or unbridled sexual desire. An intense longing.
Excess of wine: Drunkenness
Reveling: Carousels. To take intense pleasure or satisfaction.
Banqueting: Sumptuous feasts; especially elaborate and often ceremonious meals for numerous people, often in honor of a person.
Idolatries: Worship of physical objects as gods. 2: Immoderate attachment or devotion to something.

Clarke's Commentary gives pertinent information on the 6 sins listed in verse 3:

"1. They walked in lasciviousness, εν ασελγειαις· every species of lechery, lewdness, and impurity.

2. In lusts, επιθυμιαις· strong irregular appetites, and desires of all kinds.

3. In excess of wine, οινοφλυγιαις· wine, and φλυω, to be hot, or to boil; to be inflamed with wine; they were in continual debauches.

4. In revellings, κωμοις· lascivious feastings, with drunken songs, etc.

5. In banquetings, ποτοις· wine feasts, drinking matches, etc.

6. In abominable idolatries, αθεμιτοις ειδωλολατρειαις· that is, the abominations practiced at their idol feasts, where they not only worshipped the idol, but did it with the most impure, obscene, and abominable rites."

Every word in the foregoing definitions describes intoxicating agents that enslave their adherents. Peter reminded his readers that they had been freed from their former lifestyles through the sufferings of Jesus Christ.

4 Wherein they think it strange that ye run not with them to the same excess of riot, speaking evil of you:

Wherein they think it strange: They think that "*those that were clean escaped from them who live in error* (1Peter 2:18)" to be strange when they refuse to be bound anew. That reasoning would be pathetically comical to a freed slave given the choice to return to slavery. Yet, the blinded eyes of those in the grip of sin cannot perceive the realm of freedom in Jesus Christ.

5 Who shall give account to him that is ready to judge the quick and the dead.
6 For for this cause was the gospel preached also to them that are dead, that they might be judged according to men in the flesh, but live according to God in the spirit.

Wicked men and women will suffer torment in the Lake of Fire eternally. Sinners in the Old Testament will be judged on the same scale as sinners under grace will be judged. I address the subject matter of verse 6 at length in chapter 3, beginning at verse 20.

Please read my notes there.

7 But the end of all things is at hand: be ye therefore sober, and watch unto prayer.

…. end of all things is at hand: This is saying that everything that was to be determined has been determined by God An excerpt from Romans 4:17 tells us that God *"calleth those things which be not as though they were."* But that explanation describes the whole intent of the verse only partially. Peter, like Paul, apparently believed that the Lord would return to earth for His people during their lifetime. Notice this in I Thess. 4:17: *Then **we which are alive and remain** shall be caught up together with them in the clouds, to meet the Lord in the air: and so shall we ever be with the Lord.* Paul apparently believed the Lord would return while he still lived; Peter seemed to be of the same mind.

In Gen. 6:13, we read, *"God said unto Noah, The end of all flesh is come before me,"* but the end came 120 years afterward. When Peter wrote **the end of all things is at hand**, he identified things then happening and prophetically spoke of things yet to come. I believe it safe and accurate to say that Peter's words should be understood as saying, "The conclusion for all things God has instituted is predetermined.   The 2 following Scriptures demonstrate my meaning.

Ephesians 3:9: *And to make all men see what is the fellowship of the mystery, which **from the beginning** of the world hath been hid in God, who created all things by Jesus Christ:*

2Thess. 2:13: *But we are bound to give thanks alway to God for you, brethren beloved of the Lord, because God hath **from the beginning** chosen you to salvation through sanctification of the Spirit and belief of the truth:*

If a believer were given 2Thess. 2:13 only, he/she might understand the verse to deliver a message of predestination of souls. However, that understanding is refuted in the same chapter 2, verses 20,21: [20]*But in a great house there are not only vessels of gold and of silver, but also of wood and of earth; and some to honour, and some to dishonour* [21]*If a man therefore purge himself from these, he shall be a vessel unto honour, sanctified, and meet for the master's use, and prepared unto every good work.* God allows everyone a choice. From the very beginning God knew everyone that would reject Him and who would believe Him—He chose the believers **from the beginning**.

8 And above all things have fervent charity among yourselves: for charity shall cover the multitude of sins.

.... above all things: Not surprisingly, charity (selfless love) is placed as a priority in the list that Peter gave for successful Christian living. My comments on verses 9-11 follow immediately at the end of the verse with no added space between the verses:

9 Use hospitality one to another without grudging.

Hospitality: Giving of one's resources.
Grudging: To be unwilling to give or admit: give or allow reluctantly or resentfully. (M-Webster)

10 As every man hath received the gift, even so minister the same one to another, as good stewards of the manifold grace of God.

.... hath received the gift... minister (give) **the same**...*as* **good** *stewards* (bankers)... *of the* **manifold** (many; much) *grace of God.* It is impossible to give more for the cause of Christ than one receives.

11 If any man speak, let him speak as the oracles of God; if any man minister, let him do it as of the ability which God giveth: that God in all things may be glorified through Jesus Christ, to whom be praise and dominion for ever and ever. Amen.

If any man speak, let him speak as the oracles of God: The words **speak** and **minister** should not here be understood as one and the same. The oracles (authoritative precepts) of God should be included in the everyday language of Christians. A soldier's uniform shows the branch of service and the country he serves. A Christian's language shows the God he/she serves; thus, a Christian should **speak**; his/her language interlaced with the oracles of God.

…. if any man minister (if any man preaches) let him do it as of the ability which God giveth… that God be glorified in all things through Jesus Christ, to whom be praise and dominion for ever and ever. Amen. As a reader can see, key phrases from verse 11 have been grouped together and give the sense of the verse in a concise form.

In the following contribution by Gill, I believe him wrong in thinking that the word, **speak**, in verse 11 identifies **preaching**, yet he gave profound information that relates to **preaching** rather than to **speaking**:

"If any man speak, let him speak as the oracles of God: This is an application of the above general rule to a particular case, the public ministry of the word, for that is here meant: "if any man speak"; not in any manner, or on any subject; not in a private way, or about things natural and civil; but in public, and concerning divine things: "let him speak": this is rightly supplied in our translation; and in which it is supported and confirmed by the Syriac and Arabic versions, who both supply the same way: "as the oracles of God"; by which are meant the writings of the Old Testament, the sacred Scriptures; see Rom. 3:2 so called, because they come from God, are breathed and spoken by him, and contain his mind and will, and are authoritative and infallible; and according to these he is to speak who speaks in public on divine subjects, both as to the matter and manner of his speech: the matter of it must be agreeably to the divinely inspired word of God, must be fetched out of it, and confirmed by it; and he is to speak everything that is in it, and keep back nothing, but declare the whole counsel of God, and only what is in it, without mixing his own chaff, or the doctrines of men with it; and it should be spoken in a manner agreeably to it, not as the word of man, but as the word of God; and not in words which man's wisdom teacheth, but in the words of the Holy Ghost; and with all boldness, for so the Gospel ought to be spoken; and with all certainty and assurance, constantly affirming the things of it, for nothing is more sure than they are; and with all openness, plainness, and freedom, making truth manifest, laying it plain and open before men, as it ought to be; and that with all reverence and godly fear, which becomes both speaker and hearer." (Gill)

12 Beloved, think it not strange concerning the fiery trial which is to try you, as though some strange thing happened unto you:
13 But rejoice, inasmuch as ye are partakers of Christ's sufferings; that, when his glory shall be revealed, ye may be glad also with exceeding joy.
14 If ye be reproached for the name of Christ, happy are ye; for the spirit of glory and of God resteth upon you: on their part he is evil spoken of, but on your part he is glorified.

.... think it not strange concerning the fiery trial: Colloquially speaking, the phrase would say, "Don't think that the fiery trial has come upon you because you are being corrected for some fault you have committed. No, *ye are partakers of Christ's sufferings* (verse 13). You will us overwhelmed with *exceeding joy when his glory shall be revealed.* Verse 14 offers you addition support, *For the spirit of glory and of God resteth upon you...* (when) *ye be reproached for the name of Christ.* Oh, how wonderfully does our God reverse trials and testing to thrills and blessing!

15 But let none of you suffer as a murderer, or as a thief, or as an evildoer, or as a busybody in other men's matters.

As strange as it may seem that the Apostle felt it needful to pen these words to Christians, he evidently felt it necessary to alert them with the same warning that Paul wrote in 1Cor. 10:12: *Wherefore let him that thinketh he standeth take heed lest he fall.*

16 Yet if any man suffer as a Christian, let him not be ashamed; but let him glorify God on this behalf.

I know of no better way to explain Scripture than by comparing it to other Scriptures. Again, I insert an admonition by Paul, this time given to Timothy in 2Timothy 3:12: *Yea, and all that will live godly in Christ Jesus shall suffer persecution.* I think the advice from verse 12, *Beloved, think it not strange concerning the fiery trial which is to try you* should be connected with the words in this verse, *if any man suffer as a Christian.* Connected, the 2 phrases would read: *If any man suffer as a Christian, think it not strange concerning the fiery trial which is to try you.*

---

17 For the time is come that judgment must begin at the house of God: and if it first begin at us, what shall the end be of them that obey not the gospel of God?

…. Judgment: The fiery trial which is to <u>try</u> you (verse 12)
…. must begin at the house of God: Cruel trials and mocking awaited the apostles and saints of God at the very onset of the propagation of the Gospel of Jesus Christ. They were **judged** cruelly by the populace and before rulers—this is the correct interpretation for the expression, *judgment must begin at the house of God.* In this verse, notice the words, *the time is come.* Galatians 4:4, 5 identifies that **time:**

Gal 4:4*: But when the fulness of the time was come, God sent forth his Son, made of a woman, made under the law, ⁵To redeem them that were under the law, that we might receive the adoption of sons.*

There could be no judgment before Jesus came, and then **judgment** began when the Church was instituted, so **judgment began at the house of God.** Judgment in this instance in verse 17 has no relation to decision making but, rather, it identifies the time that judgment began.

18 And if the righteous scarcely be saved, where shall the ungodly and the sinner appear?

Since the righteous now are judged, tried, tested, and **barely saved**, what possible excuse could a sinner give for rejecting the blood atonement of Jesus Christ?

19 Wherefore let them that suffer according to the will of God commit the keeping of their souls to him in well doing, as unto a faithful Creator.

Wherefore let them that **suffer**… *commit the keeping of their souls to him… unto a faithful Creator.*

And let us not be weary in well doing: for in due season we shall reap, if we faint not (Galatians 6:9).

V - Feed the Flock

1 The elders which are among you I exhort, who am also an elder, and a witness of the sufferings of Christ, and also a partaker of the glory that shall be revealed:
2 Feed the flock of God which is among you, taking the oversight thereof, not by constraint, but willingly; not for filthy lucre, but of a ready mind;
3 Neither as being lords over God's heritage, but being ensamples to the flock.
4 And when the chief Shepherd shall appear, ye shall receive a crown of glory that fadeth not away.
5 Likewise, ye younger, submit yourselves unto the elder. Yea, all of you be subject one to another, and be clothed with humility: for God resisteth the proud, and giveth grace to the humble.
6 Humble yourselves therefore under the mighty hand of God, that he may exalt you in due time:
7 Casting all your care upon him; for he careth for you.
8 Be sober, be vigilant; because your adversary the devil, as a roaring lion, walketh about, seeking whom he may devour:
9 Whom resist stedfast in the faith, knowing that the same afflictions are accomplished in your brethren that are in the world.
10 But the God of all grace, who hath called us unto his eternal glory by Christ Jesus, after that ye have suffered a while, make you perfect, stablish, strengthen, settle you.
11 To him be glory and dominion for ever and ever. Amen.
12 By Silvanus, a faithful brother unto you, as I suppose, I have written briefly, exhorting, and testifying that this is the true grace of God wherein ye stand.
13 The church that is at Babylon, elected together with you, saluteth you; and so doth Marcus my son.
14 Greet ye one another with a kiss of charity. Peace be with you all that are in Christ Jesus. Amen.

Chapter 5 contains 3 exhortations, and a final salutation from Peter.
   Exhortation to elders: 1-4

Exhortation to young men: 5-7
An exhortation to remain sober and vigilant: 8-11
Salutations: 12-14

In a departure from older commentaries, and possibly from many later ones, I define the word "elders" not at all like the several I have read. My explanation follows in comments following verse 1:

1 The elders which are among you I exhort, who am also an elder, and a witness of the sufferings of Christ, and also a partaker of the glory that shall be revealed:

The word "elders" describes **age** and not **office**: An elder is not made; all men become elders if they live long enough. An elder (an old man) in a church may or may not be ordained, yet all old men in churches are elders--old men. Some elder men in churches are capable of being caretakers (deacons) of assemblies (advisors to a pastor); other elder men are capable of ministering the Word of God. It is these capable **elder** men that should **be ordained** to serve in the position that God intends them to fill—some as pastors; some as pastor associates.

.... *elders which are among you:* The word "**elders**" here means "**old** men" among you. In this verse, Peter called himself an elder, an old man. These words were written some 30 years after our Lord's ascension from Mt. Olivet. Some think that Peter was older than Jesus, which would have made him older than 33 years of age. Even if her were the same age as the Lord, and his books were written some 30 years later, Peter would have been above 60 years of age when his epistles were written. He would have been old—an elderly man—he would have been an elder—even if he had not been ordained—he was old, an elder.

An old man when he wrote to a young man, Titus, Paul gave the following instruction: *For this cause left I thee in Crete, that thou shouldest **set in order** the things that are wanting, and ordain elders in every city, as I had appointed thee* (Titus 1:5): The elders, the old men, were there already. In his feverish evangelism, Paul surged from place to place to win yet more souls to Jesus Christ. Many converts were left behind without designated leaders and preachers to guide and minister to them. Among those groups were elderly men of experience and quality, capable of teaching and guiding the congregations in correct, quality service of God. It was among that group of men that Titus was instructed to ordain as **elders**.

2 Feed the flock of God which is among you, taking the oversight thereof, not by constraint, but willingly; not for filthy lucre, but of a ready mind;
3 Neither as being lords over God's heritage, but being ensamples to the flock.

Verses 2-3, rearranged, would read as in the following:

Feed the flock *of God which is* **among** *you:* (not) ***as lords*** *over God's* **heritage** (but) *taking the oversight willingly of a ready mind; not for filthy lucre* (but be) *ensamples to the flock.*

Pastors are given the charge "to feed the flock responsibly, willingly, not governed by financial recompense, and not as being lords over God's inheritance (the church) but being willing servants of the church." Pastors often refer to the congregation they minister as "my" church. Should not that statement be altered somewhat? Too often, pastors regard themselves as bosses rather than as servants of their congregations. As a true shepherd tenderly guides and guards his flock, so should a pastor a shepherd be.

4 And when the chief Shepherd shall appear, ye shall receive a crown of glory that fadeth not away.

.... when the chief Shepherd shall appear: This beautiful phrase has never failed to thrill me when I read it. I've read this Scripture many, many times during my 71-plus years of being a Christian. I think of the many ways my **Shepherd** has led me, pushed me, shove me, turned me around, and sometimes stopped me. It was in those stopping times that I experienced discouragement, but it was then that my **Shepherd** reminded me, *But they that wait upon the LORD shall renew their strength; they shall mount up with wings as eagles; they shall run, and not be weary; and they shall walk, and not faint*

(Isaiah 40:31).

The chief Shepherd shall appear, ye shall receive a crown of glory that fadeth not away. The gospel song, "Where the Roses Never Fade" so beautifully renders this wonderful truth. There are so many things in life that fade when exposed to light. Curtains fade on windows, dark colors seem to fade rather rapidly when exposed to sunlight, but the Crowns of glory that the Chief Shepherd will give the faithful upon His return will never fade! And to think that those crowns will be exposed to the brightest Light ever for eternity! And they will never fade!

Verses 5 through 8 shift the focus from elders to young men: to their challenges, to their charges, and to their haven of hope, *the mighty hand of God* (verse 6):

5 Likewise, ye younger, submit yourselves unto the elder. Yea, all of you be subject one to another, and be clothed with humility: for God resisteth the proud, and giveth grace to the humble.

Likewise: This word gives the connotation: "As your elders have submitted themselves to the authority of God, submit yourselves to the authority of your elders." Peter's advice to the younger men in the assemblies continues with subjects related to submission. I list them in the order they are stated in this verse:

be subject one to another: The second Commandment, *Thou shalt love thy neighbor as thyself,* is here advised. *Be kindly affectioned one to another with brotherly love; in honour preferring one another,* Ron. 12:10, further explains the clause.
be clothed with humility: *Humble yourselves therefore under the mighty hand of God* (verse 6). **God giveth grace to the humble** (verse 5).
God resisteth the proud: The word, *resisteth*, should be rendered, *rejects.* To resist is to exert force in opposition to an opposing force. The word, *oppose*, would be a much better word than, resisteth. "Resisteth" leaves the idea of 2 forces, somewhat equally empowered, trying to repel one the other. Under no circumstance

can the power of evil ever be on a level equal, or even very, very remotely compared to that of God. God doesn't **resist** the force of evil—He repels it!

6 Humble yourselves therefore under the mighty hand of God, that he may exalt you in due time:

Verses 5 and 6 link together in thought. Combined, they read as follows: *Likewise, ye younger, Humble yourselves therefore under the mighty hand of God, submit yourselves unto the elder and be clothed with humility: Yea, all of you be subject one to another, for God resisteth the proud, and giveth grace to the humble.*

7 Casting all your care upon him; for he careth for you.

Casting: To cast is to throw. A person can throw **from**; can throw **to, toward, away,** and **upon.** Peter's advise for casting all care was, "Throw all your care from you, toward Jesus, and upon Jesus *"for he careth for you."* A dedicated Christian can never be taken to depths of despair that the Hand of God cannot reach him/her. In Psalm 139:8, we have these words: *If I ascend up into heaven, thou art there: if I make my bed in hell, behold, thou art there.* Never fear, O Christian, to cast *all your care upon him; for he careth for you!*

8 Be sober, be vigilant; because your adversary the devil, as a roaring lion, walketh about, seeking whom he may devour:

Be sober: Not intoxicated with *the lust of the flesh, and the lust of the eyes, and the pride of life* (1John 2L16).
be vigilant: Alertly watchful, especially to avoid danger (Merriam-Webster Collegiate Dictionary)
your adversary the devil: The devil is enemy of **all** mankind, not of Christians only, but the enemy of all mankind. An armistice, a peace treaty, can never be made with the devil. He is called Abaddon in Hebrew and Apollyon in Greek. Both words have the meaning of "destroyer".
as a roaring lion: Satan is compared to a lion in Scripture, and though he is not an actual lion, his attacks create far more havoc than that of a lion. For instance: World War II killed over 500 million people. And that's not taking into account the countless other

miseries. There were blinded eyes, missing limbs, shell-shock victims, crazed minds, congested lungs; widows, orphans, displaced persons, etc. Rightly, the devil is called a destroyer.

9 Whom resist stedfast in the faith, knowing that the same afflictions are accomplished in your brethren that are in the world.

Whom resist stedfast in the faith: Resist (fight) steadfast. (Merriam-Webster defines this word as: firmly fixed in place; immovable; not subject to change) **in the faith.** Ah, here we find the condition in which a Christian must resist—**in the faith.** *One Lord, one faith, one baptism* (Eph. 4:5).

knowing that the same afflictions: This phrase couples so closely with 1Peter 4:12: *Beloved, think it not strange concerning the fiery trial which is to try you, as though some strange thing happened unto you:* Wisely, Peter advised that the same afflictions suffered by Christians are the same as those suffered by non-Christians. What must a non-Christian think when a Christian blurts, "I can't take any more!" when he/she may be suffering the same thing? There are no quitters in the Kingdom of God.

To complete the thought intent of verse 9, I borrow from verse 10: *But the God of all grace... stablish, strengthen, settle you... make you perfect... after that ye have suffered a while.*

10 But the God of all grace, who hath called us unto his eternal glory by Christ Jesus, after that ye have suffered a while, make you perfect, stablish, strengthen, settle you.
11 To him be glory and dominion for ever and ever. Amen.

Grace is God's love extended where love is undeserved. In part, John 4:16 says: *For God so loved....* Verse 10 here gives the words: *the God of all grace.* Peter affirmed that it is that very God of all grace, all mercy, all pity, and all power that transforms sinners into saints *unto His eternal glory by* (in and through) *Christ Jesus.*

12 By Silvanus, a faithful brother unto you, as I suppose, I have written briefly, exhorting, and testifying that this is the true grace of God wherein ye stand.
By Silvanus: Most commentators agree this to be Silas. The words,

as I suppose, seem unattached to "a faithful brother" immediately preceding. I think translators should have used "assert" in place of "suppose". The sentence would then better read as: *By Silvanus, a faithful brother unto you, as I assert.*

Some think the words "by Silvanus" mean Silvanus (Silas) was Peter's copyist who actually penned Peter's words. Others think them to mean that Peter's letter was carried by Silvanus. Either or both suppositions could be correct, yet neither supposition may be true. Debate, if there be one, cannot provide an answer.

…. testifying that this is the true grace of God wherein ye stand. The Merriam-Webster Collegiate Dictionary gives the following definition for testify: to make a statement based on personal knowledge or belief: bear witness; to serve as evidence or proof. Peter had given his credentials as an eyewitness to Jesus' ministry. Now, here he **testified**—it *is the true grace of God wherein ye stand.*

13 The church that is at Babylon, elected together with you, saluteth you; and so doth Marcus my son.

Clarke's Commentary supplies the following comment on this verse: **"The Church that is at Babylon** - After considering all that has been said by learned men and critics on this place, I am quite of opinion that the apostle does not mean Babylon in Egypt, nor Jerusalem, nor Rome as figurative Babylon, but the ancient celebrated Babylon in Assyria, which was, as Dr. Benson observes, the metropolis of the eastern dispersion of the Jews….
"Instead of Babylon, some MSS. mentioned by Syncellus in his Chronicon have Ιοππη, Joppa; and one has Ρωμη, Rome, in the margin, probably as the meaning, according to the writer, of the word Babylon.
"Elected together with you - Συνεκλεκτη· Fellow elect, or elected jointly with you. Probably meaning that they, and the believers at Babylon, received the Gospel about the same time.
"And …Marcus my son - This is supposed to be the same person who is mentioned Acts 12:12, and who is known by the name of John Mark; he was sister's son to Barnabas, Col. 4:10, his mother's name was Mary, and he is the same who wrote the gospel that goes

under his name. He is called here Peter's son, i.e. according to the faith, Peter having been probably the means of his conversion. This is very likely, as Peter seems to have been intimate at his mother's house."

14 Greet ye one another with a kiss of charity. Peace be with you all that are in Christ Jesus. Amen.

Greet ye one another with a kiss of charity. Lustful men and women like the word "kiss" so long as it is not a charitable kiss— that is, a kiss with no ulterior motive attached. Secondly, the kiss here addressed is **not** a kiss on the lips. Kissing to the side of the face or neck is still practiced in greeting is several nations today. Unlike a kiss of treachery sometimes seen when enemies meet, Peter wrote of a kiss of charity; a kiss meant to convey a message of giving and devoid of lust and greed.

Peace be with you all that are in Christ Jesus. It was impossible for Peter to invoke peace for everyone, but he definitely was right when he invoked peace upon ***all that are in Christ Jesus.***

Amen. "So be it," or, "Be it so." Thank you, Brother Peter.

The Man Called Peter

Commentary on Peter's Second Epistle

I - Remembrance

1 Simon Peter, a servant and an apostle of Jesus Christ, to them that have obtained like precious faith with us through the righteousness of God and our Saviour Jesus Christ:

2 Grace and peace be multiplied unto you through the knowledge of God, and of Jesus our Lord,

3 According as his divine power hath given unto us all things that pertain unto life and godliness, through the knowledge of him that hath called us to glory and virtue:

4 Whereby are given unto us exceeding great and precious promises: that by these ye might be partakers of the divine nature, having escaped the corruption that is in the world through lust.

5 And beside this, giving all diligence, add to your faith virtue; and to virtue knowledge;

6 And to knowledge temperance; and to temperance patience; and to patience godliness;

7 And to godliness brotherly kindness; and to brotherly kindness charity.

8 For if these things be in you, and abound, they make you that ye shall neither be barren nor unfruitful in the knowledge of our Lord Jesus Christ.

9 But he that lacketh these things is blind, and cannot see afar off, and hath forgotten that he was purged from his old sins.

10 Wherefore the rather, brethren, give diligence to make your calling and election sure: for if ye do these things, ye shall never fall:

11 For so an entrance shall be ministered unto you abundantly into the everlasting kingdom of our Lord and Saviour Jesus Christ.

12 Wherefore I will not be negligent to put you always in remembrance of these things, though ye know them, and be established in the present truth.

13 Yea, I think it meet, as long as I am in this tabernacle, to stir you up by putting you in remembrance;

14 Knowing that shortly I must put off this my tabernacle, even as our Lord Jesus Christ hath shewed me.

15 Moreover I will endeavour that ye may be able after my decease to have these things always in remembrance.

16 For we have not followed cunningly devised fables, when we made known unto you the power and coming of our Lord Jesus Christ, but were eyewitnesses of his majesty.

17 For he received from God the Father honour and glory, when there came such a voice to him from the excellent glory, This is my beloved Son, in whom I am well pleased.

18 And this voice which came from heaven we heard, when we were with him in the holy mount.

19 We have also a more sure word of prophecy; whereunto ye do well that ye take heed, as unto a light that shineth in a dark place, until the day dawn, and the day star arise in your hearts:

20 Knowing this first, that no prophecy of the scripture is of any private interpretation.

21 For the prophecy came not in old time by the will of man: but holy men of God spake as they were moved by the Holy Ghost.

I find it fascinating, and puzzling at the same time, that this Book should ever have been doubted as being authoritative and as being questionable whether it be placed in the Canon. According to James MacArthur, there has been more controversary over 2ⁿᵈ Peter than over any other New Testament Book.

The Matthew Henry Commentary gives the following information:

"The apostle Peter, being moved by the Holy Ghost to write once more to those who from among the Jews were turned to faith in Christ, begins this second epistle with an introduction, wherein the same persons are described and the same blessings are desired that are in the preface to his former letter; but there are some additions or alterations which ought to be taken notice of, in all the three parts of the introduction.

"We have here a description of the person who wrote the epistle, by the name of *Simon,* as well as *Peter,* and by the title of *servant,* as well as that of *apostle. Peter,* being in both epistles, seems to be the name most frequently used, and with which he may be thought to be best pleased, it being given him by our Lord, upon his confessing *Jesus to be Christ the Son of the living God,* and the very name signifying and sealing that truth to be the fundamental article, the rock on which all must build; but the name *Simon....*"

Clarke's Commentary gives this information:

"Simon Peter - Symeon, Συμεων, is the reading of almost all the versions, and of all the most important MSS. And this is the more remarkable, as the surname of Peter occurs upwards of seventy times in the New Testament, and is invariably read Σιμων, Simon, except here, and in Acts 15:14, where James gives him the name of Symeon. Of all the versions, only the Armenian and Vulgate have Simon. But the edit. princ., and several of my own MSS. of the Vulgate, write Symon; and Wiclif has Symont.

"And an apostle - Commissioned immediately by Jesus Christ himself to preach to the Gentiles, and to write these epistles for the edification of the Church. As the writer was an apostle, the epistle is therefore necessarily canonical. All the MSS. agree in the title apostle; and of the versions, only the Syriac omits it."

1 Simon Peter, a servant and an apostle of Jesus Christ, to them that have obtained like precious faith with us through the righteousness of God and our Saviour Jesus Christ:

***Simon Peter*:** Peter identified himself in this verse with the surname, Simon, that Jesus had attached to him--Simon Peter. Peter was a definite extrovert to be sure; a man that exhibited various qualities. A fisherman by trade before Jesus called him, he emerged as a noted disciple who spoke readily; at times to be commended by the Lord, yet rebuked at other times by the Lord.

In Matt: 16:18, Jesus commended Peter for saying, " *Thou art the Christ, the Son of the living God."* In Matt. 16:23, however, the Lord said, *"Get thee behind me, Satan: thou art an offence unto me: for thou savourest not the things that be of God, but those that be of men.* After being baptized by the Holy Ghost in Acts, chapter 1, he demonstrated great power.

.... an apostle of Jesus Christ: An apostle is a "sent one." The man who had denied Jesus 3 times in the judgment hall before the rooster crowed, became the apostle to the Jews. In the third chapter of the Book of Acts, he spoke with authority and power to the man laid at the gate called Beautiful. *In the name of Jesus Christ, rise up and walk!* he commanded the beggar. Sick and impotent people were laid along the paths that Peter traveled, hoping his shadow would fall on the patient and heal him/her.

.... to them that have obtained like precious faith with us: The words, *with us,* speak of Gentile believers who shared the same Gospel with Jews who believed. They both shared *like precious faith.* Peter here referred to the "strangers and pilgrims" that he identified as Gentile believers in 1Peter, chapter 1, verse 1.

Barnes' Commentary gives the following:
"To them that have obtained like precious faith with us - With us who are of Jewish origin. This epistle was evidently written to the same persons as the former, and that was intended to embrace many who were of Gentile origin. The apostle addresses them all now, whatever was their origin, as heirs of the common faith, and as in all respects brethren."

2 Grace and peace be multiplied unto you through the knowledge of God, and of Jesus our Lord,
3 According as his divine power hath given unto us all things that pertain unto life and godliness, through the knowledge of him that hath called us to glory and virtue:

At times, translators connected modifying phrases to their subjects by using conjunctions such as **and, but,** etc. I think that to be the case with verse 2. A comma or semicolon should have been used after the word, *God,* in that verse. Eliminating the conjunction preceding the words, *Jesus our Lord,* causes the verse to read: *Grace and peace be multiplied unto you through the knowledge of God, of Jesus our Lord.* If we are to understand that the **knowledge** is imparted through God **and** through Jesus Christ, we have a problem with the personal pronoun, **his,** in verse 3. If more than 1 Person exists in the Godhead, verse 3 would read: *According as **their** divine power.*

4 Whereby are given unto us exceeding great and precious promises: that by these ye might be partakers of the divine nature, having escaped the corruption that is in the world through lust.

Whereby are given*:* "By whom they are given" is the sense of the word, *whereby.*

.... exceeding great*:* The word, exceeding, means "to an extreme degree." John 3:16 surges to the forefront when an extreme degree is encountered: *For God so loved the world, that he gave his only begotten Son, that whosoever believeth in him should not perish, but have everlasting life.*

precious *promises*: The Merriam-Webster Collegiate Dictionary describes **precious** as: of great value or high price; highly esteemed or cherished. The word appears numerous times in the New Testament:

1Cor. 3:12:	precious stones.
James 5:7:	precious fruit
1Peter 1:7:	precious faith (2Peter 1:1)
1Peter 1:19:	precious blood of Christ
1Peter 2:4:	chosen of God, and precious,
1Pe 2:6:	chief corner stone, elect, precious
1Pe 2:7	he is precious
2Peter 1:4:	precious promises
Rev. 21:11:	glory of God
Rev. 21:19	the foundations of the wall of the city

garnished with all manner of **precious** stones.

Promises*:* A promise is a **guarantee** of **fulfillment**. Words spoken as promises are empty lies when given with no intention on the part of the speaker to fulfill the "promise." A person never needs to wonder about God's promises.... *For all the promises of God in him are yea, and in him Amen, unto the glory of God by us* (2Cor. 1:20).

5 And beside this, giving all diligence, add to your faith virtue; and to virtue knowledge;

Verse 5 needs rearranging to read: *And giving all diligence beside this, add to your faith virtue; and to virtue knowledge;*

Verses 5-7 address virtues that Peter urged his readers to add. I've used Merriam-Webster for all but 3 words in the following list. The words, pure, godliness, and charity lack biblical definitions. I have supplied my own definitions for the three.

Diligence: persevering

Faith: belief; trust
Virtue: conforming to a standard of right; pure as in Chasity
Knowledge: the condition of knowing
Temperance: moderation in act, thought, or feeling
Patience: the quality of holding oneself back especially with an effort
Godliness: state of behaving as sanctioned by God
Brotherly kindness: kindness as to a brother
Charity: God on display. God is love—I John 4:8

Charity (God) produces **brotherly kindness**, displays **godliness**, gives strength to **patience** in maintaining **temperance** produced by **knowledge** of **virtuous faith.**

6 And to knowledge temperance; and to temperance patience; and to patience godliness;
7 And to godliness brotherly kindness; and to brotherly kindness charity.
8 For if these things be in you, and abound, they make you that ye shall neither be barren nor unfruitful in the knowledge of our Lord Jesus Christ.

For if these things be in you, and abound: A seed cannot reproduce unless it be planted, and it cannot reproduce bountifully without all the attributes listed in verses 5-7. But, Peter continued, **if these things** are in you and **abound**, you will be fruitful in knowledge of Jesus Christ. Not only is it necessary that **all** these be in a Christian, they must **abound** (be present in great quantity) in a Christian *that ye shall neither be barren nor unfruitful in the* **knowledge** *of our* **Lord Jesus Christ***.*

The Jamieson-Fausset-Brown Commentary on verses 5-8:
"And beside this — rather, 'And for this very reason,' namely, 'seeing that His divine power hath given unto us all things that pertain to life and godliness' (2Pet. 1:3).
"**giving** — literally, 'introducing,' side by side with God's *gift,* on your part 'diligence.' Compare an instance, 2Pet. 1:10; 2Pet. 3:14; 2Cor. 7:11.
"**all** — all possible.
"**add** — literally, 'minister additionally,' or, abundantly (compare

Greek, 2Cor.9:10); said properly of the one who *supplied* all the equipments of a chorus. So accordingly, "there will be *ministered abundantly* unto you an entrance into the everlasting kingdom of our Savior" (2Pet. 1:11).

"**to** — *Greek,* "in'; '*in* the possession of *your faith, minister virtue.* Their *faith* (answering to 'knowledge of Him,' 2Pet.1:3) is presupposed as the gift of God (2Pet.1:3; Eph. 2:8), and is not required to be *ministered* by *us; in* its exercise, *virtue* is to be, moreover, ministered. Each grace being assumed, becomes the stepping stone to the succeeding grace: and the latter in turn qualifies and completes the former. *Faith* leads the band; *love* brings up the rear [Bengel]. The fruits of *faith* specified are *seven,* the perfect number.

"**virtue** — moral excellency; manly, strenuous energy, answering to the *virtue* (energetic excellency) of God.

"**and to** — *Greek,* 'in'; 'and in (the exercise of) your virtue knowledge,' namely, practical discrimination of good and evil; intelligent appreciation of what is the will of God in each detail of practice."

9 But he that lacketh these things is blind, and cannot see afar off, and hath forgotten that he was purged from his old sins.

But he that lacketh these things is blind: The word "things" in this clause refers to the 9 necessities listed in verses 5-7 for a continuing, successful existence in Jesus Christ.

....is blind: "Has been blinded anew" is the implied sense here. Paul posted warning against falling prey to this condition in Ephesians 5:11: *And have no fellowship with the unfruitful works of darkness, but rather reprove them.* 1John 1:7 gives the formula for a successful Christian life: *But if we walk in the light, as he is in the light, we have fellowship one with another, and the blood of Jesus Christ his Son cleanseth us from all sin.*

....and hath forgotten: Unused information falls victim to newer information that eventually crowds it from the mind. Jude, verse 5 stresses the importance of remembering: *I will therefore put you in* **remembrance,** *though ye* **once knew** *this, how that the Lord, having saved the people out of the land of Egypt, afterward destroyed them that believed not.*

.... he that lacketh these things—the 9 things Peter listed as being

absolutely necessary to prevent **spiritual blindness**.

10 Wherefore the rather, brethren, give diligence to make your calling and election sure: for if ye do these things, ye shall never fall:

Wherefore: The word means, "in addition to." It is used again as the introductory word for verse 12. It summarizes the 9 things needed to follow Jesus (from diligence to charity), and that which is needed to maintain those attributes (remembrance, remembering), and the expected reward for having remembered. Verses 8, 10, and 11 complement each other.

11 For so an entrance shall be ministered unto you abundantly into the everlasting kingdom of our Lord and Saviour Jesus Christ.

.... everlasting kingdom of Jesus Christ: The Apostle Paul also wrote of an eternal kingdom in 2Cor. 5:1: *For we know that if our earthly house of this tabernacle were dissolved, we have a building of God, an house not made with hands, eternal in the heavens.*

12 Wherefore I will not be negligent to put you always in remembrance of these things, though ye know them, and be established in the present truth.

Wherefore: The same meaning as in verse 10 (in addition to). Peter again affirmed his love in that he wrote that he would not be negligent in reminding them of an ultimate, eternal reward. Peter's greatest concern, it would seem, is encapsulated in the last words of verse 12, *"and be established in the present truth."* Note Peter's fervent desire in verse 13:

13 Yea, I think it meet, as long as I am in this tabernacle, to stir you up by putting you in remembrance;

The message of verse 13 could be vocalized in the words, "It stands to reason that as long as I'm alive I will continually endeavor to keep your minds alert to the fact that you must **remember**."

14 Knowing that shortly I must put off this my tabernacle, even as our Lord Jesus Christ hath shewed me.
Knowing: An urgency in Peter's usage of this word appears manifestly. Whether he referred to the words of the Lord in John 21:18, 19; it is not known. Several commentators state that

assumption might be correct, yet also may not be correct. It is my opinion that Peter definitely remembered the Lord's statement in those verses, yet I think that he more probably referred to a special knowledge given to him by the Lord Jesus. The words, *even as our Lord Jesus Christ hath shewed me,* seem very convincing that Peter received personal knowledge from the Lord of his impending death.

15 Moreover I will endeavour that ye may be able after my decease to have these things always in remembrance.

.... after my decease: Some think that Peter may have referred to death due to his advanced age. While Peter was indeed an old man when these words were written, I doubt that he referred to his age. The statement by Peter in verse 14, *even as our Lord Jesus Christ hath* **shewed** *me,* convincing indicate that the Lord Jesus had **shown** him precisely as the Scripture in verse 14 declares.

16 For we have not followed cunningly devised fables, when we made known unto you the power and coming of our Lord Jesus Christ, but were eyewitnesses of his majesty.

.... cunningly devised fables—fairy tales—fables with which the idolatrous prophets had formerly used to deceive them.
.... when we made known unto you the power *and coming of our Lord Jesus Christ.* Heathens were not converted with fables, but in the demonstration of Power that accompanied the apostles' preaching. Peter was careful to take no credit to himself for the Power, but identified the Source in the following verses 17-18.

17 For he received from God the Father honour and glory, when there came such a voice to him from the excellent glory, This is my beloved Son, in whom I am well pleased.
18 And this voice which came from heaven we heard, when we were with him in the holy mount.

.... he received from God the Father... there came such a voice to him from the excellent glory, This is my beloved Son, in whom....

There is an enormous amount of Scripture that confirms there being One God, and that One God being the **only God**. I will not attempt to insert all the Scriptures that confirm this fact, lest I divert the intent of the highlighted phrase above. He, Jesus, received from God, the Father, a declaration from the excellent glory, that he, Jesus, was the son (the mortal) in whom the excellent dwell.

If we are to understand this verse in a physical sense as there being a son (1), a Father (2), a voice (3) excellent glory (4), then confusion follows. John 3:13 shows that the Son, standing on earth, could speak from heaven. *And no man hath ascended up to heaven, but he that came down from heaven, even the Son of man which is in heaven.*

Matthew 17:2 tells of Jesus being transfigured in the presence of Peter, James, and John. This account describes the "excellent glory" veiled in the person of Jesus Christ. Illuminated with the Glory within Him, the Voice was then heard saying, *"This is my beloved Son, in whom I am well pleased."* And to this, I add the Scripture: *To wit, that* **God was in Christ, reconciling the world** *unto himself, not imputing their trespasses unto them; and hath committed unto us the word of reconciliation (*2Cor. 5:19).

19 We have also a more sure word of prophecy; whereunto ye do well that ye take heed, as unto a light that shineth in a dark place, until the day dawn, and the day star arise in your hearts:

…. a more sure word of prophecy: This phrase gives the following connotation: "And in addition to our preaching--*when we made known unto you the power and coming of our Lord Jesus Christ, but were eyewitnesses of his majesty* (vs.16), we also have **sure** words of prophecy."
…. take heed, as unto a light that shineth in a dark place: This sentence also refers to prophecy in that it likens prophecy to a bright candle shining in a dark place:
…. the day star arise in your hearts: The Jamieson-Faucett-Brown Commentary states: "**day star** — *Greek,* the morning star," as Rev. 22:16. The Lord Jesus.

I find the words of our Lord Jesus Christ in Rev. 22:16 so very beautiful: *I Jesus have sent mine angel to testify unto you these things in the churches. I am the root and the offspring of David, and the **bright** and **morning star**.*

20 Knowing this first, that no prophecy of the scripture is of any private interpretation.

All Scripture is confirmed by other Scripture—Matt. 18:16; 2Cor. 13:1. No prophecy concerning the coming of Jesus Christ into the world was left to stand alone. Old Testament Scripture abounds with prophetic utterances of His coming.

21 For the prophecy came not in old time by the will of man: but holy men of God spake as they were moved by the Holy Ghost.

For the prophecy came not in old time - That is, in any former time, by the will of man - by a man's own searching, conjecture, or calculation; but holy men of God - persons separated from the world, and devoted to God's service, spake, moved by the Holy Ghost. So far were they from inventing these prophetic declarations concerning Christ, or any future event, that they were φερομενοι, carried away, out of themselves and out of the whole region, as it were, of human knowledge and conjecture, by the Holy Ghost, who, without their knowing anything of the matter, dictated to them what to speak, and what to write; and so far above their knowledge were the words of the prophecy, that they did not even know the intent of those words, but searched what, or what manner of time the Spirit of Christ which was in them did signify, when it testified beforehand the sufferings of Christ, and the glory that should follow." (Clarke)

II – The Dog and the Sow

1 But there were false prophets also among the people, even as there shall be false teachers among you, who privily shall bring in damnable heresies, even denying the Lord that bought them, and bring upon themselves swift destruction.

2 And many shall follow their pernicious ways; by reason of whom the way of truth shall be evil spoken of.

3 And through covetousness shall they with feigned words make merchandise of you: whose judgment now of a long time lingereth not, and their damnation slumbereth not.

4 For if God spared not the angels that sinned, but cast them down to hell, and delivered them into chains of darkness, to be reserved unto judgment;

5 And spared not the old world, but saved Noah the eighth person, a preacher of righteousness, bringing in the flood upon the world of the ungodly;

6 And turning the cities of Sodom and Gomorrha into ashes condemned them with an overthrow, making them an ensample unto those that after should live ungodly;

7 And delivered just Lot, vexed with the filthy conversation of the wicked:

8 (For that righteous man dwelling among them, in seeing and hearing, vexed his righteous soul from day to day with their unlawful deeds;)

9 The Lord knoweth how to deliver the godly out of temptations, and to reserve the unjust unto the day of judgment to be punished:

10 But chiefly them that walk after the flesh in the lust of uncleanness, and despise government. Presumptuous are they, selfwilled, they are not afraid to speak evil of dignities.

11 Whereas angels, which are greater in power and might, bring not railing accusation against them before the Lord.

12 But these, as natural brute beasts, made to be taken and destroyed, speak evil of the things that they understand not; and shall utterly perish in their own corruption;

13 And shall receive the reward of unrighteousness, as they that count it pleasure to riot in the day time. Spots they are and blemishes, sporting themselves with their own deceivings while they feast with you;

14 Having eyes full of adultery, and that cannot cease from sin; beguiling unstable souls: an heart they have exercised with covetous practices; cursed children:

15 Which have forsaken the right way, and are gone astray, following the way of Balaam the son of Bosor, who loved the wages of unrighteousness;

16 But was rebuked for his iniquity: the dumb ass speaking with man's voice forbad the madness of the prophet.

17 These are wells without water, clouds that are carried with a tempest; to whom the mist of darkness is reserved for ever.

18 For when they speak great swelling words of vanity, they allure through the lusts of the flesh, through much wantonness, those that were clean escaped from them who live in error.

19 While they promise them liberty, they themselves are the servants of corruption: for of whom a man is overcome, of the same is he brought in bondage.

20 For if after they have escaped the pollutions of the world through the knowledge of the Lord and Saviour Jesus Christ, they are again entangled therein, and overcome, the latter end is worse with them than the beginning.

21 For it had been better for them not to have known the way of righteousness, than, after they have known it, to turn from the holy commandment delivered unto them.

*22 But it is happened unto them according to the true proverb, The **dog** is turned to his own vomit again; and the **sow** that was washed to her wallowing in the mire.*

Chapter and verse arrangement continue to cause difficulty also with the starting verse of this chapter. There is no break in thought between chapter 1 and the first verse of this chapter.

1 But there were false prophets also among the people, even as there shall be false teachers among you, who privily shall bring in damnable heresies, even denying the Lord that bought them, and bring upon themselves swift destruction.

But: "But what?" It would appear at first glance that this chapter might actually be the introduction of another letter that Peter wrote. After all, the New Testament is composed from hundreds of fragments that were painstakingly put together by Bible translators. Would it have been better that the conjunction "but" to have been deleted? The answer, of course, is no. The word is needed to carry the thought from the previous chapter into this one. I include here the last verse of chapter one to demonstrate that assertion.

> *[1:21]For the prophecy came not in old time by the will of man: but holy men of God spake as they were moved by the Holy Ghost.* [2:1] **But** there were false prophets also among the people

.... there shall be false teachers among you, who privily shall bring in damnable heresies: There is but one Gospel of Jesus Christ. Anything apart from that is heresy. Among others who proclaimed there being but one Gospel message for salvation, the Apostle Paul proclaimed it so Galatians 1:8-9:

> [8] *But though we, or an angel from heaven, preach any other gospel unto you than that which we have preached unto you, let him be accursed.*
>
> [9] *As we said before, so say I now again, If any man preach any other gospel unto you than that ye have received, let him be accursed.*

.... even denying the Lord that bought them: So soon after the intense evangelism of the Gospel of Jesus Christ, the devil's recruits came forth prominently preaching a counter message: *Speaking lies in hypocrisy; having their conscience seared with a hot iron* (1Tim. 4:12);

2 And many shall follow their pernicious ways; by reason of whom the way of truth shall be evil spoken of.

And many shall follow their pernicious ways: The Merriam-Webster Collegiate Dictionary gives many definitions for, pernicious; none of them flattering:

1: highly injurious or destructive : DEADLY

2: archaic : WICKED

Synonyms: PERNICIOUS, BANEFUL, NOXIOUS, DELETERIOUS, DETRIMENTAL. All mean exceedingly harmful. PERNICIOUS implies irreparable harm done through evil or insidious corrupting or undermining *the claim that pornography has a pernicious effect on society*. BANEFUL implies injury through poisoning or destroying *the baneful notion that discipline destroys creativity*. NOXIOUS applies to what is both offensive and injurious to the health of a body or mind *noxious chemical fumes*. DELETERIOUS applies to what has an often, unsuspected harmful effect *a diet found to have deleterious effects*. DETRIMENTAL implies obvious harmfulness to something specified *the detrimental effects of excessive drinking*.

Several commentaries give, lasciviousness, as a probable interpretation for, pernicious. The 2 words are twins in meaning. I see no reason for a substitution.

3 And through covetousness shall they with feigned words make merchandise of you: whose judgment now of a long time lingereth not, and their damnation slumbereth not.

And through covetousness: To covet is to harbor a compelling desire to possess something highly unattainable and often undeserved. It is described as the lust of the eye in 1John 2:16: *For all that is in the world, the lust of the flesh, and the lust of the eyes, and the pride of life, is not of the Father, but is of the world.* Satan deftly uses all these to ensnare any and all who are not wary of his devises, and all uncomplacent people—sinner or Christian—Satan hates every person on earth.

…. with feigned words: Feigned words are words spoken as truth but imbedded with deceitful, hidden meanings.

…. make merchandise of you: They intend to purchase at little or no cost and market at exorbitant prices. False doctrines flourish through sex and money. Adherents are ensnared with feigned words, huge smiles, and smooth mannerisms of false prophets.

…. judgment now of a long time lingereth not, and their damnation slumbereth not: Though judgment and damnation for all

the false prophets of all time has lingered for a long time, it will not be delayed indefinitely. This interpretation is confirmed in the next verse:

4 For if God spared not the angels that sinned, but cast them down to hell, and delivered them into chains of darkness, to be reserved unto judgment;

For if God spared not the angels that sinned…. It is nearly impossible to imagine anyone or anything fermenting rebellion in a faultless, indescribable, perfect realm but that's exactly what Satan did. Other angels followed, and they were all cast out of heaven. Jude 1:6 speaks of that occurrence:

> *And the angels which kept not their first estate, but left their own habitation, he hath reserved in everlasting chains under darkness unto the judgment of the great day.*

…. chains of darkness: "Angels" in Jude 6 are fallen angels which are confined in a state of darkness from whence they operate. Matt. 8:12; 22:13, along with several other Scriptures in the New Testament describe a darkness, called "an outer darkness" that describes eternal punishment for the fallen angels. Jude 6 speaks of the fallen angels being **reserved** under darkness **unto** *the judgment of the great day.* It appears that Satan and all that fell with him are imprisoned in a state of darkness, and will remain so unto (until) Judgment Day. And if that assumption is indeed fact, which I believe it to be, it is no wonder that demons begged Jesus to cast them into a herd of pigs rather than to be left without sight.

5 And spared not the old world, but saved Noah the eighth person, a preacher of righteousness, bringing in the flood upon the world of the ungodly;

The Albert T. Barnes Commentary explained this verse very well: **"And spared not the old world -** The world before the flood. The argument here is, that he cut off that wicked race, and thus showed that he would punish the guilty. By that awful act of sweeping away the inhabitants of a world, he showed that people could not sin with impunity, and that the incorrigibly wicked must perish."

6 And turning the cities of Sodom and Gomorrha into ashes condemned them with an overthrow, making them an ensample unto those that after should live ungodly;

Verse 4, 5, and 6 give the same message of God's intolerance of gross wickedness and His determinate judgment against it. (1) Verse 4: Rebellious angels cast down to hell; (2) Verse 5: World completely destroyed by the Flood; (3) Verse 6: Judgment for Sodom and Gomorrha—all three verses affirm that more than one biblical witness confirms fact (see 2Cor. 13:1; 2Peter 1:20).

7 And delivered just Lot, vexed with the filthy conversation of the wicked:

8 (For that righteous man dwelling among them, in seeing and hearing, vexed his righteous soul from day to day with their unlawful deeds;)

And delivered just Lot: The words "just Lot" do not mean "only Lot". Some difficulty in understanding arises with Lot being described as "just". If consideration is given to the fact that Lot never succumbed to the constant bombarding, called vexation, for him to yield to homosexually, the word, just, might better be understood. However, Lot chose to live in Sodom, had seen more than 1 of his daughters married to sodomites, and he held some position of prominence in that city. He was reluctant to leave the city and was dragged from it by the angels. I provide an answer, however weak it may seem, following verse 9.

9 The Lord knoweth how to deliver the godly out of temptations, and to reserve the unjust unto the day of judgment to be punished:

The Lord knoweth how to deliver the godly out of temptations might translate to indicate that Abraham's intercession for Lot in the 18th chapter of Genesis won deliverance for him. Secondly, though Lot lived amid wickedness of the grossest kind, he had not succumbed to it—in that instance, he was justified.

Verse 9 compares Lot's deliverance of the righteous to the second statement-- *to reserve the unjust unto the day of judgment to be punished:*

Reserve: The word literally means "to set aside; to hold back." God is not inclined whatsoever to hasten the Day of Judgment. He was existent before time, and He will still be present when time is no more. He is not nervous in the least—it is the devils that tremble in terror (James 2:10). In God's own time *the **unjust held in reserve** will be judged and **punished**.*

10 But chiefly them that walk after the flesh in the lust of uncleanness, and despise government. Presumptuous are they, selfwilled, they are not afraid to speak evil of dignities.

But chiefly them that walk after the flesh—that is judgment is reserved (verse 9) for those who walk in the pleasures of sin in defiance to God.

.... speak evil of dignities: Merriam-Webster defines dignities as having the quality or state of being worthy, honored, or esteemed. That definitions fits well for the word in this verse. Peter's use of it was intended to identify God, angels, any of the heavenly host, **and** they that God has chosen to perform His will according to His Word.

Adam Clarke wrote the following on verse 10:

*"**But chiefly them that walk:** That is, God will in the most signal manner punish them that walk after the flesh- addict themselves to sodomitical practices, and the lust of pollution; probably alluding to those most abominable practices where men abuse themselves and abuse one another."*

I find it amazing that a man, whose works were published **200 years' ago**, could find the practice of sodomy so detestable and revolting as to warrant the judgment of God. God condemned sodomy such an ungodly sin as to warrant the total destruction of Sodom, Gomorrah, all the cities of the plain, and every inhabitant of that area except Lot and his 2 daughters to death. How can His hatred for that sin now go unnoticed? Adam Clarke understood it

200 years ago—what punishment must await those who ignore God!
I return now to Clarke's Commentary for additional comments on this verse:

"Despise government: They brave the power and authority of the civil magistrate, practicing their abominations so as to keep out of the reach of the letter of the law; and they speak evil of dignities-they blaspheme civil government, they abhor the restraints laid upon men by the laws, and would wish all governments destroyed that they might live as they list.

"Presumptuous are they: tolmhtai. They are bold and daring, headstrong, regardless of fear.

"Self-willed: auyadeiv. Self-sufficient; presuming on themselves; following their own opinions, which no authority can induce them to relinquish.

"Are not afraid to speak evil of dignities: They are lawless and disobedient, spurn all human authority, and speak contemptuously of all legal and civil jurisdiction. Those in general despise governments, and speak evil of dignities, who wish to be under no control, that they may act as freebooters in the community."

11 Whereas angels, which are greater in power and might, bring not railing accusation against them before the Lord.

Whereas.... The word delivers the connotation of "as evidence against." It is evidence against [1]walking is the lust of the flesh, [2]the despisers of government, [3]presumption,[4] self-will; and [5]they who speak evil against dignities—all listed in verse 10. Jude 1:8-11 gives a second witness against all who engage in such practices:

> [8]*Likewise also these filthy dreamers defile the flesh, despise dominion, and speak evil of dignities.*

> [9]*Yet Michael the archangel, when contending with the devil he disputed about the body of Moses, durst not bring against him a railing accusation, but said, The Lord rebuke thee.*

> [10]*But these speak evil of those things which they know not: but what they know naturally, as brute beasts, in those things they corrupt themselves.*

> [11]*Woe unto them! for they have gone in the way of Cain, and*

ran greedily after the error of Balaam for reward, and perished in the gainsaying of Core.

12 But these, as natural brute beasts, made to be taken and destroyed, speak evil of the things that they understand not; and shall utterly perish in their own corruption;

But these: Though this expression might be understood to be addressing sinners in general, that is not the message that Peter intended. He didn't veer from the subject that he introduced in the first 2 verses of this chapter. I insert those 2 verses from this very chapter here for easy reference:

> *2Peter 2:1: [1]But there were false prophets also among the people, even as there shall be false teachers among you, who privily shall bring in damnable heresies, even denying the Lord that bought them, and bring upon themselves swift destruction.*
>
> *[2]And many shall follow their pernicious ways; by reason of whom the way of truth shall be evil spoken of.*

…. as natural brute beasts….domestic animals…. **made to be taken and destroyed**….animals raised to be slaughtered for human consumption. Peter's message is clear: the false prophets mouthed false doctrine as though they had no human intelligence.

…. shall utterly perish in their own corruption: Peter compared the false prophets to unclean animals not fit for human consumption. He said, "As a donkey will die and rot where it falls, so will false teachers be destroyed by their own corruptible teachings."

Gill wrote a very descriptive excerpt for verse 12:

"But these, as natural brute beasts,…. So far are these men from acting like the angels, that they are sunk below their own species, and are like beasts, and become brutish in their knowledge and behaviour; are like the horse and the mule, without understanding, act as if they were without reason; yea, are more stupid and senseless than the ox, or the ass, which know their owner, and their crib; and even in those things which they might, and do know by the light of nature, they corrupt themselves; and being given up to judicial blindness, and a reprobate mind, call good evil, and evil good, and do things that are not convenient, and which even brute beasts do not; and like as they are guided by an instinct in nature, to do what they do, so these men are led and influenced by the force and power of corrupt nature in them, to commit all manner of wickedness:"

13 And shall receive the reward of unrighteousness, as they that count it pleasure to riot in the day time. Spots they are and blemishes, sporting themselves with their own deceivings while they feast with you;

And shall receive the reward of unrighteousness: Death is a certainty for **everything**, for humans, for animals, birds, reptiles, plants, etc. Infidels who deny there being a God, still make wills, purchase life insurance and burial plots because they know they will **die**. But it is **God** Who asserted in Heb. 9:27: *And as it is **appointed** unto men once to die, **but** after this **the judgment**:* St. John 5:28,29 delivers the same message: *Marvel not at this: for the hour is coming, in the which all that are in the graves shall hear his voice, [29]And shall come forth; they that have done good, unto the resurrection of life; and they that have done evil, unto the resurrection of damnation.*

14 Having eyes full of adultery, and that cannot cease from sin; beguiling unstable souls: an heart they have exercised with covetous practices; cursed children:

Several commentaries render about the same meaning for this passage. I've chosen Barnes' comments to include here. I find them very profound and insightful:

"**Having eyes full of adultery** - Margin, as in the Greek, 'an adulteress;' that is, gazing with desire after such persons. The word 'full' is designed to denote that the corrupt passion referred to had wholly seized and occupied their minds. The eye was, as it were, full of this passion; it saw nothing else but some occasion for its indulgence; it expressed nothing else but the desire. The reference here is to the sacred festival mentioned in the previous verse; and the meaning is, that they celebrated that festival with licentious feelings, giving free indulgence to their corrupt desires by gazing on the females who were assembled with them. In the passion here referred to, the 'eye' is usually the first offender, the inlet to corrupt desires, and the medium by which they are expressed. The wanton glance is a principal occasion of exciting the sin; and there is much often in dress, and mien, and gesture, to charm the eye and to deepen the debasing passion.

"And that cannot cease from sin - They cannot look on the females who may be present without sinning. Compare Matt. 5:28. There are many men in whom the presence of the most virtuous woman only excites impure and corrupt desires. The expression here does not mean that they have no natural ability to cease from sin, or that they are impelled to it by any physical necessity, but only that they are so corrupt and unprincipled that they certainly will sin always.

"Beguiling unstable souls - Those who are not strong in Christian principle, or who are naturally fluctuating and irresolute. The word rendered beguiling means to bait, to entrap, and would be applicable to the methods practiced in hunting. Here it means that it was one of their arts to place specious allurements before those who were known not to have settled principles or firmness, in order to allure them to sin. Compare 2Tim. 3:6.

"An heart they have exercised with covetous practices - Skilled in the arts which covetous men adopt in order to cheat others out of their property. A leading purpose which influenced these men was to obtain money. One of the most certain ways for dishonest men to do this is to make use of the religious principle; to corrupt and control the conscience; to make others believe that they are eminently holy, or that they are the special favorites of heaven; and when they can do this, they have the purses of others at command. For the religious principle is the most powerful of all principles; and he who can control that, can control all that a man possesses. The idea here is that these persons had made this their study, and had learned the ways in which men could be induced to part with their money under religious pretenses. We should always be on our guard when professedly religious teachers propose to have much to do with money matters. While we should always be ready to aid every good cause, yet we should remember that unprincipled and indolent men often assume the mask of religion that they may practice their arts on the credulity of others, and that their real aim is to obtain their property, not to save their souls.

"Cursed children - This is a Hebraism, meaning literally, "children of the curse," that is, persons devoted to the curse, or who will certainly be destroyed."

15 Which have forsaken the right way, and are gone astray, following the way of Balaam the son of Bosor, who loved the wages of unrighteousness;
16 But was rebuked for his iniquity: the dumb ass speaking with man's voice forbad the madness of the prophet.

Which have forsaken the right way: This expression was not intended to address sinners in general—it directly attacks the false teachers who troubled the Church at that time. Satan uses many devices for confusion in both sinners and Christians. He is wily, treacherous, and evil beyond description. A seemingly favorite tool for him to use is to mix, to adulterate, truth with fiction, with lies. Truth mixed with lies = **all** lie. During the temptation of Jesus, the devil tried to force the Lord to reveal His identity prematurely. "For it is written," he said, "cast yourself down (from the top of the Temple) for He shall give His angels charge over you….and they will bear you up---they will catch you." Beware, O Christian, lest you fall victim to this ruse!

The way of Balaam - Is the counsel of Balaam. He counselled the Moabites to give their most beautiful young women to the Israelitish youth, that they might be enticed by them to commit idolatry. See Num. 22:5; 23:1 (Clarke)

Balaam counselled the Moabites to entice the children of Israel to illicit connection with their women, thus introducing licentiousness into the camp of the Hebrews (Numbers 31:16; compare Numbers 25:1-9); and in like manner these teachers led others into licentiousness, thus **corrupting** the church. (Barnes)

17 These are wells without water, clouds that are carried with a tempest; to whom the mist of darkness is reserved for ever.

These are wells without water: False prophets still are here addressed. Empty messaging containing no eternal truth.

…. clouds that are carried with a tempest: This describes fury likened unto a cyclone or tornado that wreak indescribable damage.

The tragedy of this application is that it here speaks of soul destruction rather than physical damage. First Peter 4:8 pettingly describes **the tempest**;

> *Be sober, be vigilant; because your adversary the devil, as a roaring lion, walketh about, seeking whom he may devour.*

18 For when they speak great swelling words of vanity, they allure through the lusts of the flesh, through much wantonness, those that were clean escaped from them who live in error.

…. they speak great swelling words: Beautiful, smooth speeches impregnated with enticement

…. they allure through the lusts of the flesh: 1John 2:16 warns: *For all that is in the world, the lust of the flesh, and the lust of the eyes, and the pride of life, is not of the Father, but is of the world.*

…. through much wantonness: Peter here used "much wantonness" to emphasize the depth of the evil that the false prophets used to deceive and snare unsuspecting people, especially Christians. I think the word "wanton" needs a very thorough explanation. I use the Merriam-Webster Collegiate Dictionary to supply the following definitions:

> 1 a archaic: hard to control: UNDISCIPLINED, UNRULY b: playfully mean or cruel : MISCHIEVOUS
>
> 2 a: LEWD, BAWDY   b: causing sexual excitement : LUSTFUL, SENSUAL
>
> 3 a: MERCILESS, INHUMANE *wanton cruelty* b: having no just foundation or provocation : MALICIOUS *a wanton attack*
>
> 4: being without check or limitation: as a: luxuriantly rank *wanton vegetation* b: unduly lavish: EXTRAVAGANT

I'm convinced that Peter would have agreed with the Merriam-Webster definition for "wanton". A very real danger here, however, is that Peter stated "**much** wantonness." There is end to the devil's attack on all humanity.

…. those that were clean escaped: First Corinthians 10:12 gives valuable warning to all Christians, lest they fall victim to Satan's

ruses: *Wherefore let him that thinketh he standeth take heed lest he fall.*

19 While they promise them liberty, they themselves are the servants of corruption: for of whom a man is overcome, of the same is he brought in bondage.

While they promise them liberty: Smooth talking, deceptive preaches persuade unsuspecting Christians into thinking that they are restricted by the rules and doctrines of their church. They preach liberty—freedom—shake off the bonds of organized religion—be free! The thing that is actually happening in that type situation is free Christians, like freed slaves, are being snared by the net of the devil and again made slaves--slaves then to Satan.

Clarke's Commentary gives a good definition for "slave" in this verse:

"For of whom a man is overcome - This is an allusion to the ancient custom of selling for slaves those whom they had conquered and captivated in war. The ancient law was, that a man might either kill him whom he overcame in battle, or keep him for a slave. These were called *servi*, slaves, from the verb *servare*, to keep or preserve. And they were also called *mancipia*, from *manu capiuntur*, they are taken captive by the hand of their enemy. Thus, the person who is overcome by his lusts is represented as being the slave of those lusts."

20 For if after they have escaped the pollutions of the world through the knowledge of the Lord and Saviour Jesus Christ, they are again entangled therein, and overcome, the latter end is worse with them than the beginning.

21 For it had been better for them not to have known the way of righteousness, than, after they have known it, to turn from the holy commandment delivered unto them.

For if after they have escaped..., *they are again entangled... the latter end is worse with them than the beginning.* Hebrews 6:4-6 places a dire warning for this type situation:

[4]For it is impossible for those who were once enlightened, and have tasted of the heavenly gift, and were made

partakers of the Holy Ghost,

⁵And have tasted the good word of God, and the powers of the world to come,

⁶If they shall fall away, to renew them again unto repentance; seeing they crucify to themselves the Son of God afresh, and put him to an open shame.

I find it disappointing that several commentaries remain largely silent on the subject of "falling away." I understand that the subject remains debatable within religious circles. I think it not applicable to a weak Christian who has not been convinced of the full impact of the Power of God. Yet, conversely, a Christian who has truly been born again and felt the full impact of the Power of God, to turn about and scorn God and His Word to the point of blasphemy—to him/her, there is no chance for repentance. They become worse than they were before they were originally forgiven for their sin.

22 But it is happened unto them according to the true proverb, The dog is turned to his own vomit again; and the sow that was washed to her wallowing in the mire.

I'm including a quote from Barnes' Commentary that, in my mind, is an almost complete misunderstanding of this verse:

But it is happened unto them according to the true proverb - The meaning of the proverbs here quoted is, that they have returned to their former vile manner of life. Under all the appearances of reformation, still their evil nature remained, as really as that of the dog or the swine, and that nature finally prevailed. There was no thorough internal change, any more than there is in the swine when it is washed, or in the dog. This passage, therefore, would seem to demonstrate that there never had been any real change of heart, and of course there had been no falling away from true religion. It should not, therefore, he quoted to prove that true Christians may fall from grace and perish. The dog and the swine had never been anything else than the dog and the swine, and these persons **had never been anything else than sinners.**"

Barnes' contention that this verses names sinners who "had never been anything else than sinners" is proved **totally wrong** by verse **20: ....** *they have* **escaped** *the pollutions of the world through the* **knowledge of the Lord** *and Saviour Jesus Christ:* His allusion to a dog and a sow behaving like dogs and sows naturally behave misses its intent. A dog or a sow **cannot** be changed. Peter referred to people **saved...***through the* **knowledge of the Lord** *and Saviour Jesus Christ.*

III – Where is the Promise of His Coming?

1 This second epistle, beloved, I now write unto you; in both which I stir up your pure minds by way of remembrance:

2 That ye may be mindful of the words which were spoken before by the holy prophets, and of the commandment of us the apostles of the Lord and Saviour:

3 Knowing this first, that there shall come in the last days scoffers, walking after their own lusts,

*4 And saying, **Where is the promise of his coming?** for since the fathers fell asleep, all things continue as they were from the beginning of the creation.*

5 For this they willingly are ignorant of, that by the word of God the heavens were of old, and the earth standing out of the water and in the water:

6 Whereby the world that then was, being overflowed with water, perished:

7 But the heavens and the earth, which are now, by the same word are kept in store, reserved unto fire against the day of judgment and perdition of ungodly men.

8 But, beloved, be not ignorant of this one thing, that one day is with the Lord as a thousand years, and a thousand years as one day.

9 The Lord is not slack concerning his promise, as some men count slackness; but is longsuffering to us-ward, not willing that any should perish, but that all should come to repentance.

10 But the day of the Lord will come as a thief in the night; in the which the heavens shall pass away with a great noise, and the elements shall melt with fervent heat, the earth also and the works that are therein shall be burned up.

11 Seeing then that all these things shall be dissolved, what manner of persons ought ye to be in all holy conversation and godliness,

12 Looking for and hasting unto the coming of the day of God,

wherein the heavens being on fire shall be dissolved, and the elements shall melt with fervent heat?

13 Nevertheless we, according to his promise, look for new heavens and a new earth, wherein dwelleth righteousness.

14 Wherefore, beloved, seeing that ye look for such things, be diligent that ye may be found of him in peace, without spot, and blameless.

15 And account that the longsuffering of our Lord is salvation; even as our beloved brother Paul also according to the wisdom given unto him hath written unto you;

16 As also in all his epistles, speaking in them of these things; in which are some things hard to be understood, which they that are unlearned and unstable wrest, as they do also the other scriptures, unto their own destruction.

17 Ye therefore, beloved, seeing ye know these things before, beware lest ye also, being led away with the error of the wicked, fall from your own steadfastness.

18 But grow in grace, and in the knowledge of our Lord and Saviour Jesus Christ. To him be glory both now and forever. Amen.

Chapter 3 does not flow chronologically; that is, all the verses are not arranged in the order the events listed in them will transpire. I think this to be intentional and ordained so by God. 1Cor. 2:14 states: *But the natural man receiveth not the things of the Spirit of God: for they are foolishness unto him: neither can he know them, because they are spiritually discerned.*

It would at first appear from his first 2 words of verse 1 of this chapter, that Peter here introduced another epistle altogether. That is not the case, however. In this chapter, the reader will notice instances where the Apostle addressed both Christian Jews and Christian Gentiles. All this is in addition to what he previously had written in this epistle.

1 This second epistle, beloved, I now write unto you; in both which I stir up your pure minds by way of remembrance:

I stir up your pure minds: The words "your **pure** minds" tell us that Peter here addressed Christians exclusively. In previous chapters of both of his letters, Peter spoke largely to Gentile converts. In this verse, however, there is little doubt that he addressed Christian Jews as well as Gentile converts.

2 That ye may be mindful of the words which were spoken before by the holy prophets, and of the commandment of us the apostles of the Lord and Saviour:

That ye may be mindful of the words which were spoken before by- -two witnesses: (1) holy prophets, (2) the apostles of Jesus Christ. Every great truth in God's Word is confirmed by more than 1 witness, that is; by 2 or more Scriptures (see Matt: 18:16; 2Cor. 13:1; 2Peter 1:20).

3 Knowing this first, that there shall come in the last days scoffers, walking after their own lusts,
*4 And saying, **Where is the promise of his coming?** for since the fathers fell asleep, all things continue as they were from the beginning of the creation.*

Knowing this first: Peter does not here say that the **first** thing to mark the last days is scoffers. He intended the meaning to be, "You need to know this first." He then proceeded to name signs of the last days. If this verse stood alone, it could be applied to many periods of time in the Christian era. But the verse does not stand alone. Scoffers in the last day are identified by the taunting question they ask in verse 4.

5 For this they willingly are ignorant of, that by the word of God the heavens were of old, and the earth standing out of the water and in the water:
6 Whereby the world that then was, being overflowed with water, perished:
.... willingly are ignorant: There is no excuse for ignorance. Peter's words indicate that this type of ignorance is one of rebellion

—they willingly--they wanted to--they intended to remain ignorant. They refused to be instructed by the Word of God that as the world had previously been destroyed by a universal flood, so would it again be destroyed.

7 But the heavens and the earth, which are now, by the same word are kept in store, reserved unto fire against the day of judgment and perdition of ungodly men.

…. heavens and the earth: "Heavens" in this verse speak of the sun, moon, stars, and all the constellations. None of this was destroyed by the Flood. All of it will be destroyed prior to the great White Throne Judgment of God.

…. which are now: This phrase delivers the message of: the heavens, sun, moon, stars, and the earth we stand on.

…. by the same word: This phrase refers to Genesis 1:1: *In the beginning God created the heaven and the earth.*

…. are kept in store: The heavens and the earth you now see are held in place and reserved by the same Word of the same One and Only God.

8 But, beloved, be not ignorant of this one thing, that one day is with the Lord as a thousand years, and a thousand years as one day.

…. one day is with the Lord: Time is immaterial with God. He is not governed by the rising and setting of the Sun. When the Sun's light is extinguished, God will not be left in darkness. He doesn't have to mark off days on the calendar after each setting sun. But let it never be said that God will ever forget a promise to bless the faithful and to judge the disobedient.

9 The Lord is not slack concerning his promise, as some men count slackness; but is longsuffering to us-ward, not willing that any should perish, but that all should come to repentance.

I include here an excerpt from a lengthy article on this verse from Barnes' commentary:

"The Lord is not slack concerning his promise - That is, it should not be inferred because His promise seems to be long delayed that therefore it will fail. When people, after a considerable lapse of time, fail to fulfil their engagements, we infer that it is because they have changed their plans, or because they have forgotten their promises, or because they have no ability to perform them, or because there is a lack of principle which makes them fail, regardless of their obligations. But no such inference can be drawn from the apparent delay of the fulfillment of the divine purposes. Whatever may be the reasons why they seem to be deferred, with God, we may be sure that it is from no such causes as these.

"As some men count slackness - It is probable that the apostle here had his eye on some professing Christians who had become disheartened and impatient, and who, from the delay in regard to the coming of the Lord Jesus, and from the representations of those who denied the truth of the Christian religion, arguing from that delay that it was false, began to fear that his promised coming would indeed never occur. To such he says that it should not be inferred from his delay that he would not return, but that the delay should be regarded as an evidence of his desire that men should have space for repentance, and an opportunity to secure their salvation.

"But is long-suffering to us-ward - Toward us. The delay should be regarded as a proof of His forbearance, and of His desire that all human beings should be saved. Every sinner should consider the fact that he is not cut down in his sins, not as a proof that God will not punish the wicked, but as a demonstration that He is now forbearing, and is willing that he should have an ample opportunity to obtain eternal life. No one should infer that God will not execute His threats, unless he can look into the most distant parts of a coming eternity, and demonstrate that there is no suffering appointed for the sinner there; anyone who sins, and who is spared even for a moment, should regard the respite as only a proof that God is merciful and forbearing now.

"Not willing that any should perish - That is, He does not desire it or wish it. His nature is benevolent, and He sincerely desires the eternal happiness of all, and His patience toward sinners "proves" that He is willing that they should be saved. If He were not willing, it would be easy for Him to cut them off, and exclude them from hope immediately."

10 But the day of the Lord will come as a thief in the night; in the which the heavens shall pass away with a great noise, and the elements shall melt with fervent heat, the earth also and the works that are therein shall be burned up.

But the day of the Lord: This phrase denotes 3 different events to come upon all the earth:
1. It speaks of the catching up of the Church, known in religious circles as the Rapture, in Matt. 24:43; Luke 12:39; 1Thess. 5:2. It is vividly described in 1Thess. 4:14-18.
2. It speaks of a great tribulation time.   There are many Scriptures throughout the Word of God that allude to this event. I refer to Isiah 51:6 for Old Testament prophecy, and to Hebrews 1:11 for New Testament prophecy on the same subject.
3. It speaks of final judgment and the destruction of all creation. Peter wrote of this in this verse 10 with the words, *the heavens shall pass away with a great noise, and the elements shall melt with fervent heat, the earth also and the works that are therein shall be burned up.*

In my research for authoritative sources for explanation on this verse, I discovered a missive written by Adam Clarke in his Commentary. Adam Clarke (1760 or 1762 - 1832) was a British Methodist theologian and Biblical scholar. He is chiefly remembered for writing a commentary on the Bible which took him 40 years to complete and which was a primary Methodist theological resource for two centuries. I do not here endorse nor condemn the man or his religious affiliation. However, I find the interpretation of this verse by a man who **died** nearly 200 years ago very interesting.

Clarke:
"The heavens shall pass away with a great noise: As the heavens mean here, and in the passages above, the whole atmosphere, in which all the terrestrial vapors are lodged; and as water itself is composed of two gases, eighty-five parts in weight of oxygen, and fifteen of hydrogen, or two parts in volume of the latter, and one of

the former; (for if these quantities be put together, and several electric sparks passed through them, a chemical union takes place, and water is the product; and, vice versa, if the galvanic spark be made to pass through water, a portion of the fluid is immediately decomposed into its two constituent gases, oxygen and hydrogen;) and as the electric or ethereal fire is that which, in all likelihood, God will use in the general conflagration; the noise occasioned by the application of this fire to such an immense congeries of aqueous particles as float in the atmosphere, must be terrible in the extreme. Put a drop of water on an anvil, place over it a piece of iron red hot, strike the iron with a hammer on the part above the drop of water, and the report will be as loud as a musket; when, then, the whole strength of those opposite agents is brought together into a state of conflict, the noise, the thunderings, the innumerable explosions, (till every particle of water on the earth and in the atmosphere is, by the action of the fire, reduced into its component gaseous parts,) will be frequent, loud, confounding, and terrific, beyond every comprehension but that of God himself.

"**The elements shalt melt with fervent heat:** When the fire has conquered and decomposed the water, the elements, **stoiceia**, the hydrogen and oxygen airs or gases, (the former of which is most highly inflammable, and the latter an eminent supporter of all combustion,) will occupy distinct regions of the atmosphere, the hydrogen by its very great levity ascending to the top, while the oxygen from its superior specific gravity will keep upon or near the surface of the earth; and thus, if different substances be once ignited, the fire, which is supported in this case, not only by the oxygen which is one of the constituents of atmospheric air, but also by a great additional quantity of oxygen obtained from the decomposition of all aqueous vapors, will rapidly seize on all other substances, on all terrestrial particles, and the whole frame of nature will be necessarily torn in pieces, and thus the earth and its works be burned up."

11 Seeing then that all these things shall be dissolved, what manner of persons ought ye to be in all holy conversation and godliness,

In verse 9, Peter presented the surety of the promises of God for those who patiently wait for them. In verse 10, he alluded to surprise. Surprise is an element applicable to both the Rapture and the suddenness of judgment upon earth's remaining wicked people. Consecrated Christians look for signs for these events—those who don't look will be surprised.

…. all these things shall be dissolved: A better understanding of the intent of this verse might result from the substitution of "so because" for "seeing," making the statement read: (So, because) *all these things shall be dissolved, what manner of persons ought ye to be in all holy conversation and godliness,.* The verse ends with a comma rather than a question mark, with which it should have ended. Peter intended that they understand that all temporal thing shall be destroyed and nothing left but God. He asked, "what manner?" or how should they conduct themselves in the fear of God. When everything is dissolved, destroyed, Peter reasoned, there's nothing left except God. But to please God, her furthered reasoned, requires a total surrender to Him.

12 Looking for and hasting unto the coming of the day of God, wherein the heavens being on fire shall be dissolved, and the elements shall melt with fervent heat?

Looking for and hasting unto: I think the connotation here is well expressed in the last clause of Romans 8:26: *…. but the Spirit itself maketh intercession for us with groanings which cannot be uttered.* Barnes submitted that the Greek rendered the meaning: "hasting the coming." The Greek word rendered "hasting," (σπεύδω speudō,) means to urge on, to hasten; and then to hasten after anything, to await with eager desire. I believe this to be the desire of every fervent Christian. Rev. 22:20 delivers the feeling of eager anticipation in the hearts Christians for the Lord's return for His Church. They find needed strength in Jesus' words: *He which testifieth these things saith, Surely, I come quickly.* **Amen.** *Even so,* **come***, Lord Jesus*

13 Nevertheless we, according to his promise, look for new heavens and a new earth, wherein dwelleth righteousness.

Nevertheless: This word can be understood as: "but" or: "in view of the final destruction of all things."

Insurance companies offer policies for nearly every imaginable thing. None of them can offer insurance for eternal life. That insurance, that assurance, was paid for by the Lord's death on the cross and His resurrection from death. Peter was an eyewitness of the Lord's death, and an eyewitness of His resurrected body. It is with authority that he wrote, *according to his promise, look for new heavens and a new earth, wherein dwelleth righteousness.*

.... new heavens and a new earth, wherein dwelleth righteousness: Various opinions within religious circles are offered as explanations for this phrase. "New heaven" **and** "new earth" are a unit in which **righteousness** dwells. It is not here said that holiness reigns in this new heaven but only righteousness reigns on a new earth. May we view this phrase with the understanding of the original creation of heaven and earth, Genesis 1:1:

In the beginning God created the heaven and the earth.

Genesis 1:1 identifies "earth" as the one we stand on and "heaven" as that which we look upward to see during day and night. Neil Armstrong proved that man can and did stand on the moon, which Adam would have viewed as being in the heaven. The New Heaven and the New Earth should be understood in the same sense as the original creation; that is, not as 2 separate places. **Righteousness** will reign throughout the New Creation---not holiness in heaven and righteousness in a distant New Earth.

14 Wherefore, beloved, seeing that ye look for such things, be diligent that ye may be found of him in peace, without spot, and blameless.

Verse 14 is incomplete without the first phrase of verse 15. A complete verse would read: *14 Wherefore, beloved, seeing that ye look for such things, be diligent that ye may be found of him in peace, without spot, and blameless, 15And account that the longsuffering of our Lord is salvation.*

Peter's intention here might well be worded as: "Beloved, since you embrace this hope, be very conscious that you walk circumspectly before God, knowing *that the longsuffering of our Lord* is your guarantee of *salvation."*

15 And account that the longsuffering of our Lord is salvation; even as our beloved brother Paul also according to the wisdom given unto him hath written unto you;

16 As also in all his epistles, speaking in them of these things; in which are some things hard to be understood, which they that are unlearned and unstable wrest, as they do also the other scriptures, unto their own destruction.

.... even as our beloved brother Paul:

The Jamieson-Fausset-Brown Commentary supplies very pertinent information on this phrase:

"also in all his epistles — Rom 2:4 is very similar to 2Pe 3:15, beginning. The Pauline Epistles were by this time become the *common* property of all the churches. The "all" seems to imply they were now completed. The subject of the Lord's coming is handled in 1Th_4:13; 1Th_5:11; compare 2Pe 3:10 with 1Th 5:2. Still Peter distinguishes Paul's Epistle, or Epistles, "TO YOU," from "*all* his (*other*) Epistles," showing that certain definite churches, or particular classes of believers, are meant by "you."

"in which — *Epistles.* The oldest manuscripts read the feminine relative (hais); not as Received Text (hois), "in which *things.*"

"some things hard to be understood — namely, in reference to Christ's coming, for example, the statements as to the man of sin and the apostasy, before Christ's coming. "Paul seemed thereby to delay Christ's coming to a longer period than the other apostles, whence some doubted altogether His coming" [Bengel]. Though there be some things hard to be understood, there are enough besides, plain, easy, and sufficient for perfecting the man of God. "There is scarce anything drawn from the obscure places, but the same in other places may be found most plain" [Augustine]. It is our own prejudice, foolish expectations, and carnal fancies, that make Scripture difficult [Jeremy Taylor].

"unlearned — Not those wanting *human* learning are meant, but those *lacking the learning imparted by the Spirit.* The humanly *learned* have been often most deficient in spiritual learning, and have originated many heresies. Compare 2Ti 2:23, a different *Greek* word, "unlearned," literally, "untutored." When religion is studied as a science, nothing is more abstruse; when studied in order to know our duty and practice it, nothing is easier.

"unstable — not yet established in what they have learned; shaken by every seeming difficulty; who, in perplexing texts, instead of waiting until God by His Spirit makes them plain in comparing them with other Scriptures, hastily adopt distorted views.

"wrest — strain and twist (properly with a *hand screw*) what is straight in itself (for example, 2Ti 2:18).

"other scriptures — Paul's Epistles were, therefore, by this time, recognized in the Church, as "Scripture": a term never applied in any of the fifty places where it occurs, save to the Old and New Testament sacred writings. Men in each Church having miraculous *discernment of spirits* would have prevented any uninspired writing from being put on a par with the Old Testament word of God; the apostles' lives also were providentially prolonged, Paul's and Peter's at least to thirty-four years after Christ's resurrection, John's to thirty years later, so that fraud in the canon is out of question. The three first Gospels and Acts are included in "the other Scriptures," and perhaps all the New Testament books, save John and Revelation, written later.

"unto their own destruction — not through Paul's fault (2Peter 2:1)."

17 Ye therefore, beloved, seeing ye know these things before, beware lest ye also, being led away with the error of the wicked, fall from your own steadfastness.

Paul's words in First Corinthians 10:12, *Wherefore let him that thinketh he standeth take heed lest he fall,* affirm the importance of Peter's words in this verse-- *beware lest ye also, being led away--- fall from your own steadfastness.* Steadfastness in the faith can be maintained if strict attention is given to the words in the next verse.

18 But grow in grace, and in the knowledge of our Lord and Saviour Jesus Christ. To him be glory both now and forever. Amen.

Moths are attracted to bright lights, and when they approach, the warmth of the light causes the wing of the moth closest to the light to beat more rapidly than the other wing. The faster-beating wing pulls the moth into a circle, which causes the inner wing to beat faster still, pulling the moth ever closer to the light. As the circular path becomes tighter and tighter, the moth eventually crashes onto the light and to its death. Oh, may every Christian approach that *Light which lighted every man that cometh into the world* (John 1:9) until they die out completely to the power of sin's allure! AMEN!